REVISE FOR RELIGIOUS STUDIES GCSE

AQA B

Key Beliefs, Ultimate Questions and Life Issues

Peter Smith
David Worden

heinemann.co.uk
✓ Free online support
✓ Useful weblinks
✓ 24 hour online ordering

01865 888058

Heinemann
Inspiring generations

Heinemann Educational Publishers
Halley Court, Jordan Hill, Oxford OX2 8EJ
Part of Harcourt Education

Heinemann is the registered trademark of
Harcourt Education Limited

© David Worden and Peter Smith 2003

First published 2003

08 07 06 05 04 03
10 9 8 7 6 5 4 3 2 1

British Library Cataloguing in Publication Data is available
from the British Library on request.

ISBN 0 435 30702 9

Copyright notice
All rights reserved. No part of this publication may be reproduced in any form or by any means (including photocopying or storing it in any medium by electronic means and whether or not transiently or incidentally to some other use of this publication) without the written permission of the copyright owner, except in accordance with the provisions of the Copyright, Designs and Patents Act 1988 or under the terms of a licence issued by the Copyright Licensing Agency, 90 Tottenham Court Road, London W1T 4LP. Applications for the copyright owner's written permission should be addressed to the publisher.

Designed by Artistix
Typeset by TechType, Abingdon, Oxon

Original illustrations © Harcourt Education Limited, 2003

Illustrated by TechType, Abingdon, Oxon
Printed in the UK by Bath Press
Cover photo © Science Photo Library

The publishers would like to thank the following for the use of copyright material: LIFE for the logo on p. 42 © LIFE Education www.lifeuk.org; NAC for the logo on p. 42 © National Abortion Campaign nac.gn.apc.org

The publishers would like to thank the following for permission to reproduce photographs: p. 13, 18, 29 (top) Andes Press Agency; p. 28 Science & Society Picture Library; p. 29 (bottom) Alamy/ David Sanger; p. 32 (top right and left), p. 35 Alamy; p. 32 (bottom) Getty; p. 37 Corbis; p. 41, 53, 58 SPL; p. 48 David Hoffman/ Alamy; p. 59 Panos/Frank Hoogervorst

Acknowledgements
Every effort has been made to contact copyright holders of material reproduced in this book. Any omissions will be rectified in subsequent printings if notice is given to the publishers.

There are links to relevant websites in this book. In order to ensure that the links are up-to-date, that the links work, and that the sites are not inadvertantly linked to sites that could be considered offensive, we have made the links available on the Heinemann website at www.heinemann.co.uk/hotlinks. When you access the site the express code is **7029P**.

Tel: 01865 888058   www.heinemann.co.uk

Contents

How to use this book 4

Section A: Key beliefs

1. Buddhism 6
2. Christianity 9
3. Hinduism 12
4. Islam 15
5. Judaism 18
6. Sikhism 21
7. Christian ethics: Attitudes to love and forgiveness 24

Section B: Questions of meaning

8. The existence of God 27
9. The problem of suffering 31
10. Life after death 35

Examination questions 39

Section C: Life issues

11. Abortion 41
12. War and peace 44
13. Prejudice and discrimination 47

Examination questions 50

Section D: Planet earth

14. The origins of life 52
15. Human attitudes towards animals 55
16. The care of the planet 58

Examination questions 61

Glossary 63

Index 64

How to use this book

Revise for Key Beliefs, Ultimate Questions and Life Issues Specification B Module 2 has been written to help you revise successfully for your Religious Studies GCSE.

Your course

Module 2, Key Beliefs, Ultimate Questions and Life Issues is divided into four sections.

Section A is divided into seven questions; you are required to answer just one complete question. This section tests knowledge and understanding of Christianity, Buddhism, Hinduism, Islam, Judaism, Sikhism *or* Christian Ethics. Section B examines questions of meaning – the existence of God, suffering and life after death. Section C looks at life issues – abortion, prejudice and war. Section D explores religious attitudes towards creation, the care of the environment and animals. For sections B, C and D you choose one out of two complete questions.

Which religious tradition?

In Section A you are required to answer a question using one religion. For the rest of the exam you may use one or two religions in any one answer. The choice is yours but on the paper as a whole you are not allowed to use more than three religions. It might be a good idea to use the same religion throughout the paper. If you are using just one religion for Sections B, C and D try to include different viewpoints within that religion. For example, in answering an abortion question using Christianity you could discuss how Roman Catholics are opposed to abortions in all circumstances but Methodists will allow it if it is regarded as the lesser of two evils.

An example of a multi-faith approach might be:

- Section A – Key Beliefs – Islam
- Section B – Question on suffering – Buddhism
- Section C – Question on War – Christianity and Islam
- Section D – Question on the environment – Christianity

The exam paper

The time allowed for this paper is 1 hour 45 minutes. During this time you are required to answer four questions. Questions will be divided into several parts, so make sure you answer every part. In Section A select one question out of the seven. In the other sections choose one out of the two questions set and answer all parts of the questions you have selected.

Do not forget to read each question carefully before you start to answer it. You need to relate the information you know directly to the question being asked. Each question is marked out of 20 and the maximum mark for the paper is 83. You will be awarded up to 3 marks for quality of written communication (QWC). Good QWC marks will be awarded if you:

- ensure that your writing is legible (use a blue or black ink or ball-point pen) and spell, punctuate and use grammar correctly
- use religious technical terms where appropriate
- use a suitable structure and style of writing, for example write in sentences and paragraphs.

Quotations

Learn two or three quotations from sacred texts or general religious principles and, if appropriate, one statement or teaching by a religious leader or authority. Some examples will be given in this book, but you should use the ones you have spent two years studying. Do not waste time trying to learn unfamiliar texts.

How this book is organized

Each section begins with 'What do I need to know?' which outlines information you will need to answer examination questions on the topic.

Margin features

Did you know?
Short pieces of information that are useful additions to your knowledge and can be used as examples in examination answers.

Hints and tips
Brief guidelines designed to assist revision and examination technique.

Exam watch
Brief tips to help you achieve better marks in your exam.

Beware
Tips to help you avoid commonly made mistakes in the exam.

Key ideas
Short points that summarize the main points in a section.

Action point
Brief exercises that you can practise to help you revise.

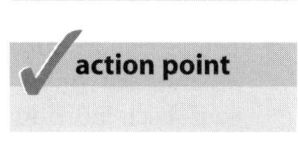

Read more
Suggestions for further reading to help you add more detail to your answers. These may also direct you to another section of the book where passages or topics are explained in more detail.

Key words

Important words and terms are in bold print the first time they appear in the book. Definitions can be found in the Glossary on pages 63–4. You should learn these and be prepared to explain them.

Questions

Each section ends with practice questions with the number of marks in brackets. This guides how much you should write.

Mark	Requirement
1	Write a simple one-word answer or a short sentence
2	'Give *two* reasons…' = write two simple points 'Explain…' = make one simple point with a sentence to explain it
3	Make one simple point, explain it and give an example
4 or more	Write continuously (see below)

Questions worth 4 marks or more are usually marked on levels of response. The examiner decides which level you reached in your answer and awards the marks attached to that level.

Questions worth 5 marks (evaluation questions) usually begin with a controversial statement and ask, 'Do you agree? Give reasons for your answer, showing that you have thought about more than one point of view.' Some also say, 'Refer to religious teachings in your answer.' These are always marked on levels of response. You cannot reach Levels 4 and 5 unless you refer to more than one point of view. You cannot reach Level 5 without referring to at least one religious argument.

SECTION A: KEY BELIEFS

1 Buddhism

What do I need to know?
- The significance of Siddattha Gotama.
- The nature and importance of the Tipitaka.
- The Three Marks of Existence.
- The Three Refuges.
- The Four Noble Truths.
- The Five Precepts.
- The Eightfold Path.
- The goal of **nibbana**.
- **Worship** and **meditation** in Buddhism.

did you know? Buddhism is a way of life founded on the teachings of Siddattha Gotama (the Buddha). Buddhists do not worship Buddha, as they do not believe in God.

Siddattha Gotama

Born in Lumbini, near the Himalayan foothills in the sixth century BCE, Siddattha Gotama was brought up as a prince. On chariot rides from the palace, the suffering he saw shocked him. These sights were:

- old age
- illness
- death
- a holy man.

Challenged by this suffering, he left his life of luxury and endured extreme hardship for six years. Having failed to find an answer to suffering, he meditated under the bodhi tree until he became 'enlightened'. Then he taught others until his death at Kusinara.

The Tipitaka (the three baskets or Pali Canon)

These holy writings are divided into:

- The Vinaya Pitaka (discipline): the purest collection of the Buddha's teachings
- The Sutta Pitaka (themes): the central teachings of Theravada Buddhism (includes the Dhammapada)
- The Abhidhamma Pitaka: explains the teachings of the Sutta Pitaka.

key ideas
By studying texts Buddhists learn about their religion. Texts are chanted in worship to bring positive effects.

The Three Marks of Existence or Three Universal Truths

The Buddha taught that:

- everything changes (**anicca**). Nothing lasts forever.
- people change (**anatta**). Anatta means 'no separate self' or 'no permanent identity or soul'. Each individual is made up of five factors (khandhas): consciousness (sankhara), feelings (vedana), thoughts (vijnana), sight or perception (samina), and the physical body (rupa). From birth to death we are always changing.
- life is unsatisfactory and involves suffering (**dukkha**).

The Three Refuges (Jewels)

Buddhists believe in the authority of the Buddha, the dhamma and the sangha. At the beginning of their devotions they recite: 'I go to the Buddha for my refuge. I go to the teaching (dhamma) for my refuge. I go to the order (sangha) for my refuge.'

The Four Noble Truths

- **Dukkha**: Life is unsatisfactory and three 'poisons' lead to more suffering, namely ignorance, greed and hatred.
- **Tanha**: Desire or craving. Tanha is the attempt to grasp at the things we enjoy.
- **Niroda**: The cure for suffering – get rid of desire and craving and then you do not suffer any more.
- **Magga**: The Buddha said to follow the Middle Way between the extremes of luxury and real hardship. This is set out in the Eightfold Path.

The Eightfold Path

This path can be divided into three main parts: wisdom (panna), morality (sila) and mental development (samadhi).

did you know? Each of the steps of the Eightfold Path begins with the word 'right'. This means 'best possible'.

The way of wisdom

- Right viewpoint: The right viewpoint means understanding the meaning of the Four Noble Truths.
- Right intention: The right intention is the positive thought that leads to actions that are unselfish. The intention is to care about others, rather than concentrating on oneself.

The next three steps give Buddhists guidance on behaviour.

The way of morality

- Right speech: Speech should be kind, gentle, truthful, not hurtful and helpful.
- Right action: Buddhists try to live by the Five Precepts.

  'I undertake to abstain from:
  taking life (killing)
  taking what is not freely given (stealing)
  the misuse of the senses (misusing sex)
  wrong speech (lying)
  taking drugs and alcohol which cloud the mind.'

- Right living: People should earn their living in a useful occupation that does not involve hurting others.

The way of mental development

- Right effort: Train the mind to avoid negative things and to dwell on good positive things like love and peace.
- Right mindfulness: People need to be aware of happenings around them and within. This awareness is helped by meditation.
- Right concentration: Minds should be trained to 'let go' of unwanted thoughts and become calm and peaceful.

> **key ideas**
> The ultimate goal is to become free of the cycle of birth, death and rebirth, and to enter nibbana (the eternal state or peace that is beyond suffering).

Worship (puja)

Worship can occur at anytime, anywhere. Some Buddhists worship at the shrine in their home, others at the temple. Theravada Buddhists do not pray during worship but Mahayana Buddhists pray to bodhisattas for help in their lives.

Shrines

The shrines vary according to the different branches of Buddhism. Objects include:

- a statue or picture of the Buddha
- a bell to announce the next step in puja or meditation
- candles (symbol of enlightenment)
- flowers (symbol of anicca)
- food (offerings)
- incense (symbolizes the spread of the dharma throughout the world)
- photographs of Buddhist teachers or dead ancestors
- sacred texts (these may be chanted)

- toba (wooden tablets are offered in memory of the dead)
- water (water is valuable and life giving; a sign of reverence and respect).

key ideas
The worship includes chanting, making offerings, listening to the scriptures and reciting short passages.

Aids to worship

Prayer wheels
Prayer wheels can be handheld or fixed and contain mantras. The wheels are spun so that good vibrations are sent in all directions.

Mala or juzu
The juzu or mala beads are used to count the times a mantra has been recited.

key ideas
Meditation is an attempt to empty the mind of all thoughts. Negative thoughts are replaced with thoughts of peace and tranquillity.

Metta meditation
Metta (loving kindness) meditation aims to cultivate friendly and warm feelings towards living things.

Samatha meditation
This enables the mind to become calm, alert and focused on one object or idea. Buddhists become aware of their breathing and peace and joy arises in them.

Vipassana meditation
This enables a person to gain insight. It is practised by sitting in the lotus position and involves looking at your mind as if observing it from outside.

Short questions
a Who became known as the Buddha? (1 mark)
b What does dukkha mean? (1 mark)

Examination practice
a Name *two* objects seen at a shrine. (2 marks)
b Explain the importance of meditation. (5 marks)

Checklist for revision

	Understand and know	Need more revision	Do not understand
I know how Buddhism started and the importance of Siddattha Gotama.	☐	☐	☐
I understand the importance of the Tipitaka.	☐	☐	☐
I understand the main ideas of Buddhist teaching including the Four Noble Truths and the Eightfold Path.	☐	☐	☐
I know about Buddhist worship and meditation.	☐	☐	☐

SECTION A: KEY BELIEFS

2 Christianity

What do I need to know?
- How Christianity began.
- Christianity today.
- The life of Jesus.
- The significance of the Bible.
- The nature of God.
- Beliefs about salvation and eternal life.
- The importance of the resurrection.
- Liturgical and non-liturgical worship.
- The significance of Holy Communion.

did you know? Christianity began about 2000 years ago in Israel. Over 1½ billion people are Christians.

Jesus

Jesus was born in Bethlehem, the son of Mary. King Herod tried to kill him but Mary and Joseph took him to Egypt. When Herod died they returned to Nazareth. Aged 30, Jesus was baptized by John the Baptist. He chose twelve disciples and began preaching and performing **miracles**. Three years later he was crucified but rose from the dead three days later.

God

Christians believe in one God known in three persons (**The Holy Trinity**) – the Father, the Son (Jesus), and the Holy Spirit (Holy Ghost). They believe that:

- God the Father is the creator of the universe and He sustains life
- Jesus, God's only Son, became incarnate – God took human form and lived on earth
- the Holy Spirit guides believers to do the right thing and comforts and helps them through life.

did you know? Matthew, Mark, Luke and John recorded the life of Jesus in the first four books of the New Testament (Gospels). The Christian holy book, the Bible, is divided into the Old Testament (before the birth of Jesus) and the New Testament. It is studied as the Word of God.

Salvation and eternal life

key ideas
Possessions can become an idol and prevent people from obtaining eternal life.

Luke 18: 18–30

A rich ruler asked Jesus how to obtain eternal life. Jesus' reply involved keeping the Ten Commandments and putting God first in life. Jesus told him to give his money to the poor but he was unwilling to do this. Jesus said, 'It is much harder for a rich man to enter the Kingdom of God than for a camel to go through the eye of a needle.'

key ideas
Jesus' mission was to save lost sinners.

Luke 19: 1–10

At Jericho, Jesus went to a chief tax collector's (Zacchaeus') house. The people grumbled because Zacchaeus was a sinner, but the visit changed his life. Zacchaeus promised that he would give half his belongings to the poor and pay back four times as much to the people he had cheated. Jesus saw Zacchaeus' repentance and said, 'Salvation has come to this house.'

The resurrection (Luke 24: 1–12)

Early on Sunday morning (Easter Day), some women, including Mary Magdalene, Joanne and Mary the mother of James, took spices to embalm Jesus' body. The tomb entrance stone had been removed and Jesus' body was gone. Two men (angels) said that Jesus had risen from the dead. Terrified, they returned to tell the Apostles. Peter ran to the tomb and found only the linen wrappings.

The walk to Emmaus (Luke 24: 13–49)

A stranger joined Cleopas and his friend as they walked from Jerusalem to Emmaus. They did not recognize the stranger even though he explained the prophecies about how the Messiah would die. At Emmaus, as the stranger broke the bread, Cleopas and his friend realized it was Jesus. They returned to Jerusalem to be told that Jesus had appeared to Simon.

Jesus appeared, ate some fish and commanded that the message about repentance and the forgiveness of sins be preached everywhere.

The purpose and significance of the resurrection

Christians believe that:

- as a perfect sacrifice, Jesus paid the price for sin to be forgiven
- only Jesus was good enough to be the atonement for sin
- it is proof that Jesus is God's Son and there is eternal life
- everyone needs to know the good news
- it has inspired millions, even to endure persecution.

1 Corinthians 15: 12–22

St Paul wrote a letter to the Christians at Corinth and explained that:

- Christianity is based on the resurrection
- if it did not happen then Christians are to be pitied
- if it is not possible for people to be raised to life then Jesus is still dead
- as Jesus did conquer death then believers will have eternal life.

Worship

key ideas

Christians worship God in many different ways. Some prefer quiet and a time of reflection, others enjoy clapping, singing and dancing.

Some denominations have liturgical (a set form) worship. A service book may be used (for example, Roman Catholics use the Missal) and the congregation read the written responses. Worship may be full of ritual (symbolic actions).

Some Christians prefer liturgical worship because:

- it becomes familiar
- it is easily followed
- the ritual is enjoyed
- the emphasis on the sacraments is enjoyed
- they know what is going to happen next.

Non-liturgical worship has no set form. Prayers are made up on the spot – this is known as *extempore* prayer. A worship group may lead the praise and worship.

Some Christians prefer non-liturgical worship because:

- it is unpredictable and interesting
- each service is different
- it is less formal
- people can express themselves more in their worship
- the Holy Spirit guides the worship.

Holy Communion

At the Last Supper before his crucifixion, Jesus asked his followers to eat bread and drink wine to remember his sacrifice.

2 Christianity

> **key ideas**
> The bread represents Jesus' broken body and the wine his blood, which cleanses people from sin.

In most Christian denominations Holy Communion (the Eucharist, Divine Liturgy or Mass) is the central act of worship. Roman Catholics believe that the bread and wine mysteriously changes into the body and blood of Jesus. This belief is called transubstantiation.

Short questions

a What does 'incarnation' mean? (1 mark)

b How was Jesus put to death? (1 mark)

Examination practice

a What do Christians receive at Holy Communion? (2 marks)

b Why do some people prefer non-liturgical worship? (5 marks)

Checklist for revision

	Understand and know	Need more revision	Do not understand
I know about the life of Jesus.	☐	☐	☐
I understand the importance of the Bible.	☐	☐	☐
I understand Christian teaching about salvation and eternal life.	☐	☐	☐
I know the story of the resurrection and understand its importance for Christians.	☐	☐	☐
I know about different forms of Christian worship.	☐	☐	☐

SECTION A: KEY BELIEFS

3 Hinduism

> **What do I need to know?**
> - The origins of Hinduism.
> - The nature and significance of **shruti** and **smriti** scriptures.
> - The concept of Brahman.
> - The concept of atman.
> - Some of the Hindu deities.
> - Hindu teachings and concepts.
> - Worship and meditation in Hinduism.

Origins

Hinduism does not have an historical founder. Its origin may go back some 4,500 years to the Indus Valley and the Aryan culture in Northern India.

did you know? Hinduism has no creed, is not prophetic, has no single moral code, and no specific holy writing that is the real authority.

The scriptures

These are divided into shruti and smriti.

Shruti means 'that which is heard' and was revealed to the ancient seers. It cannot be changed. The Rig Veda is the oldest and was passed down orally. The four main collections are called the Vedas: Rig Veda, Sama Veda, Yajur Veda, and Atharva Veda. They are written in Sanskrit. 'Veda' means 'knowledge'.

Smriti means 'that which is remembered'. These do not have the same authority as the shruti scriptures and can be added to. They include the Purana, the Mahabharata and Ramayana, The Laws of Manu, Tantras and Darshana literature.

Brahman and atman

Brahman is the ultimate reality, the universal supreme spirit that is eternal and unchanging. Brahman is present everywhere in everything. Brahman's presence in each person is called atman. This is the 'self' or 'soul' and is eternal. When the body dies, the atman takes another body and returns to another life. Eventually the soul finds reunion with Brahman as it breaks out of the cycle of reincarnation.

> **key ideas**
> Hinduism is a religion with many deities, but Hindus believe they are all different aspects of Brahman.

The triad of deities

The Trimurti consists of Brahma, Vishnu and Shiva.

Brahma

Brahma is the creator of the universe. Images show Brahma with four faces, sitting on a lotus flower, holding a rosary, a gourd (a bowl made from gourd fruit) and a book.

Vishnu

Vishnu is the protector/preserver who comes to the earth in different forms to overthrow evil. Images show him holding a shell, a discus, a lotus and a mace. He is often painted blue. Vishnu appeared on earth in ten avatars (incarnations): the fish, the tortoise, the boar, the man-lion, the dwarf, Parashu Rama with an axe, Rama, Krishna, the Buddha and Kalki.

Shiva

The destroyer and a god of fertility, his city is Varanasi and images show him with at least four hands. As Lord of the Dance, Shiva dances on the back of the dwarf of ignorance and controls the universe's movement. He has a serpent around his neck, a necklace of skulls, the crescent moon in his hair, a trident, a rosary, and is holding a gourd. Shiva wears a tiger skin and snake collar and rides the bull Nandi.

Other deities

Rama

The story of Rama is told in the Ramayana. An

avatar of Vishnu, Rama represents an obedient son, a devoted husband, a king who fulfils his duty, and a brave warrior.

Krishna

Krishna played naughty tricks on people when he was a child, for example, on the gopis (milkmaids). Disguised as a charioteer, he advised Arjuna on the eve of battle.

Ganesha (Ganapati)

The son of Shiva, Ganesha is the god of wisdom and knowledge who removes obstacles. He was beheaded by Shiva's trident and received the head of an elephant. Images show him with four arms and hands: a snare is in one, a goad (a pointed stick) and an axe in another, sweetmeats in the third, and the fourth hand blesses worshippers.

Lakshmi

The wife of Vishnu, she is the goddess of love, prosperity and good fortune. Images show her as a woman of beauty and gentleness, seated on a lotus flower and rewarding worshippers with gold.

Kali

The wife of Shiva, images show her as fierce and bloodthirsty with a necklace of skulls and a skirt of severed hands.

The four aims of life

Dharma

Dharma means doing your religious duties and avoiding doing wrong. It helps in acquiring good karma or merit.

Artha

Artha means to obtain a job and earn a living. The goal is to be successful in work and contribute to the economic development of society.

Kama

Kama is controlled pleasure, including enjoyment of the senses and sexual pleasure.

Moksha

Reaching **moksha** is the goal for Hindus and results from the liberation from samsara.

> **key ideas**
>
> **Ahimsa** means having respect for life and not using violence; for example, most Hindus are vegetarians.
>
> **Karma** means work or actions – you reap what you sow. Good actions bring good karma and its reward of a good future life. Bad actions bring a life of suffering.
>
> **Samsara** is the term given to the cycle of birth, life, death and rebirth.

Worship in Hinduism

Puja

Each home has a shrine with an image of the deity who is worshipped. Daily offerings are given and mantras are said. A puja tray contains the items used – flowers, fruit, incense stick, water, milk, ghee lamp, rice-grains, red kum-kum powder and yellow turmeric powder.

Mala

This is a string of 108 beads used while repeating the name of the deity and while saying the word 'Aum'.

The mandir or temple

Offerings of food, money or flowers are made here. Shoes are removed as a bell is rung to wake up the deities and Hindus sit facing the shrine. Pandits (priests) bathe the murti and dress them in royal robes and flowers. Bhajans (hymns) are sung and often worshippers dance. The priest pours ghee into the fire during prayers. An arti tray is moved before the image of the deity. It contains symbols of the five elements – fire, earth, air, ether and water. Worshippers receive prashad (sacred food).

Meditation, yoga and mantra

Hindus meditate as an aid towards reaching moksha. Many chant a mantra with a specific rhythm in order to get a deity to help them reach their goal. They may use a yantra (external object or symbol) to help their concentration.

Many Hindus practise yoga as it helps them gain control over their body and mind. Control of selfishness, greed and anger enables the person to seek union with the universal spirit and so escape samsara.

Short questions

a What is artha? (1 mark)

b What is ahimsa? (1 mark)

Examination practice

a Name *two* objects found on a puja tray. (2 marks)

b 'The home is the most important place of worship.' Do you agree? (5 marks)

c Explain the importance of meditation. (5 marks)

Checklist for revision

	Understand and know	Need more revision	Do not understand
I understand the importance of the Hindu scriptures.	☐	☐	☐
I understand the concepts of Brahman and atman.	☐	☐	☐
I know about the main Hindu deities.	☐	☐	☐
I understand the four aims of life.	☐	☐	☐
I understand the concepts of ahimsa, karma and samsara.	☐	☐	☐
I know about Hindu worship and meditation.	☐	☐	☐

SECTION A: KEY BELIEFS

4 Islam

What do I need to know?
- The origins of Islam.
- The significance of Muhammad.
- The nature and significance of the Qur'an.
- The attributes of Allah.
- The concept of **tawhid**.
- Beliefs about life after death.
- The Five Pillars of Islam.

did you know?
- The word 'Islam' means 'submission' or 'surrender' to Allah (God).
- Followers of Islam are Muslims ('one who has surrendered to Allah').
- There are over 1 billion Muslims in the world.
- There are two main streams – Sunni (the largest) and Shi'ite.

beware
Do not call Muslims 'Islams'.

Origins

Muslims believe that Islam has always existed. Prophets gradually revealed the faith to humanity, for example Adam, Ibrahim (Abraham), Musa (Moses), Dawud (David) and Isa (Jesus). The final and complete revelation was given to Muhammad in the seventh century.

key ideas
Muhammad is known as the seal (the last and greatest) of the prophets.

Muhammad's life
- Born in **Makkah**, Saudi Arabia in 570 CE.
- Married his employer, a wealthy widow, called Khadijah.
- Deeply spiritual, he spent time alone, praying and meditating.
- When aged 40, the Night of Power (Laylat-ul-Qadr) occurred in a cave on Mount Hira. The angel Jibril (Gabriel) appeared to Muhammad with words from Allah (God).
- Further revelations took place over a period of more than twenty years.
- Muhammad recited these words from Allah to friends who wrote them down. All together they form the Qur'an.
- In 620 CE, the angel Jibril took Muhammad to Jerusalem (the Night Journey). He was carried on a winged horse like the creature called al-Buraq. Muhammad ascended to heaven, saw God's throne, and spoke to the prophets.
- Muhammad then preached about Allah but was not well received in Makkah.
- In 622 CE he went to Madinah. This is known as the Hijrah (departure).
- In 630 CE he conquered Makkah and in 632 CE he died in Madinah.

key ideas
The Qur'an is known as 'the mother of all books' (as it is Allah's words).

The Qur'an
- The Qur'an is written in Arabic with 114 surahs (chapters).
- Each surah (except one) begins with 'In the name of Allah, the Compassionate, the Merciful.'
- The shari'ah (Islamic Law) is based on the Qur'an.

- The Qur'an is treated with great respect – Muslims wash before reading it.
- It is kept on a high shelf, covered and dust free.
- Children learn Arabic so they can read it.

did you know? The Hadith contains the sayings, instructions and reports of actions of Muhammad.

key ideas
Muslims believe in one God, Allah – nothing is equal to Him. This belief is called tawhid (the oneness of God).

did you know? The Qur'an reveals the 99 names of Allah.

The attributes of Allah

Allah is described as the Compassionate, the Merciful, Lord of the Universe (The Qur'an, surah 1); Sovereign Lord, the Holy One, the Giver of Peace, the Keeper of Faith, the Guardian, the Mighty One, the All-powerful, the Most High, the Creator, the Originator, the Modeller, the Wise One (The Qur'an, surah 59).

beware
It is forbidden to regard anything as equal to Allah (the sin of 'shirk'). Images, statues or pictures of Allah are forbidden.

key ideas
All people earn, or are responsible for, their own salvation. Peoples characters are tested.

The afterlife

Life after death is called **akhirah**. It lasts forever (eternity). The angel of death takes souls to **barzakh** (a state of waiting). Then, on the **Day of Judgement**, two angels open a book of all our actions. After judgement, the saved walk over the Assirat Bridge to paradise and the wicked fall off to hell.

Paradise (heaven) is described as a wonderful green garden with flowers and the sound of water and birdsong. **Jahannam** (hell) is described as a horrible place of torment, where the damned will be chained amid hot winds, boiling water and black smoke.

key ideas
Islam is a complete way of life.

The Five Pillars of Islam

These are the essential practices or duties that every believer must fulfil.

1. Shahadah: the declaration of belief – 'I witness that there is no other God but Allah, and Muhammad is the prophet of Allah.'

2. Salah(t): Muslims pray five times a day. The **muezzin** calls the faithful to prayers from the minaret (tower). Praying together in **mosques** confirms the brotherhood or **Ummah**. Muslims perform **wudu** (ritual washing) before praying. **Rak'ahs** (ritual movements) are performed, led by the imam. All face towards the **Ka'bah** in Makkah.

3. Zakah: is giving money to charity. This is usually two and a half per cent of a Muslim's annual savings. It goes towards helping the poor, building hospitals, and so on.

4. Saum: During the ninth month (Ramadan) Muslims fast. Those over twelve (except the sick, elderly, pregnant women, those breast-feeding or travellers) do not eat or drink during daylight hours.

4 Islam

5 Hajj: Muslims try to go on pilgrimage to Makkah at least once in their lifetime. Pilgrims wear white cloth to show equality. At the Great Mosque they circle the Ka'bah seven times (tawaf). Some kiss the black stone. They run seven times between two hills, Safa and Marwah. They remember Hagar and Ishmael and visit the Zamzam Well. At Mount Arafat (The Mount of Mercy), they meditate from noon until sunset. At Mina, stones are collected to throw at three pillars (these represent the devil). The Id-ul-Adha feast is the climax of the pilgrimage and lasts for four days. Once back in Makkah, the pilgrims circle the Ka'bah seven times.

Short questions

a What does the word 'Islam' mean? (1 mark)

b Name *two* of the Five Pillars of Islam. (2 marks)

Examination practice

a Give *two* of the attributes of Allah. (2 marks)

b Explain the importance of the Qur'an. (5 marks)

c Explain the importance of zakah (charity) to Muslims. (5 marks)

Checklist for revision

	Understand and know	Need more revision	Do not understand
I know how Islam started and the importance of Muhammad.	☐	☐	☐
I understand the concept of tawhid and some of the attributes of Allah.	☐	☐	☐
I understand Muslim beliefs about what happens after death.	☐	☐	☐
I know the Five Pillars of Islam.	☐	☐	☐

SECTION A: KEY BELIEFS

5 Judaism

> **What do I need to know?**
> - The origins of Judaism.
> - The nature and importance of the Tenakh.
> - Beliefs about God.
> - The Covenant.
> - Repentance, Rosh Hashanah and Yom Kippur.
> - Kashrut.
> - Shabbat and its importance.

The beginnings

Many claim that Judaism started with Abraham, as he represents the first man to believe in one God (monotheism). God made many promises to Abraham including that he would have many descendants and they will become a great nation.

Moses is regarded as the Law-giver. He led the Jews out of slavery in Egypt to the Promised Land and he received the Ten Commandments from God on Mount Sinai. King David crushed the power of the Philistines and expanded the land held by the Jews.

The Covenant

A covenant is an agreement. God made covenants with several people including Moses. He said that the Jews would be His 'chosen people'. In return they were to worship Him alone and obey the commandments.

The Tenakh

The Jewish scriptures are known as the Tenakh. This is made up of the Torah (Law), Nevi'im (The Prophets) and Ketuvim (Writings).

The Torah

The most sacred part of scripture, it contains the early history of the Jews, the 613 mitzvot (commandments), the Ten Commandments, and the Noachide code. It is handwritten on scrolls. Their parading and reading is a very important part of Jewish worship. The Torah is treated with great respect as the revealed Word of God.

The Nevi'im

These books of the prophets continue the history of the Jews from the death of Moses, for example, Joshua, Judges, Samuel, Kings, Isaiah, Jeremiah and Ezekiel.

Ketuvim

These writings contain more of the history, for example, Esther, Daniel and Nehemiah. The Psalms are a collection of prayers, songs and praises of God. Proverbs gives advice for moral living and Ecclesiastes and Job are concerned with the meaning of life and suffering. Ruth is a story of romance and The Song of Songs is a love poem.

Jewish beliefs about God

Jews believe in one God (monotheism). God is seen as the creator and sustainer of the universe.

God as judge

God is a righteous judge who protects and blesses the Jews when they are faithful to Him. If they forget God and break His laws then they can expect punishment. God is their redeemer and they look forward to the day when He will rule the world.

> **did you know?** Repentance means saying sorry for your sins and being determined to change your behaviour.

Rosh Hashanah

Rosh Hashanah is the New Year festival lasting for two days. At morning worship, the shofar (ram's horn) is blown 100 times. This calls people to prayer and repentance for their wrongdoing. It is seen as a time of judgement when God reviews their actions over the past year. He then decides what will happen to them during the next year. Jews bless each other with the words, 'May you be written down for a good year.' Special foods are eaten, for example, slices of apple dipped in honey.

The Ten Days of Awe follow when God gives people the chance to repent and atone (make up). Some give to charity, some throw breadcrumbs into a river (a symbol of getting rid of their sins).

Yom Kippur

Yom Kippur is the most holy and solemn day of the year. God closes and seals the Book of Life. Those who have repented properly will receive a good year. Jews fast for 25 hours and confess their sins. There are five services in the synagogue and it is the custom to wear white (symbolizes purity).

The Shema

The Shema is the most important Jewish prayer which begins with the words, 'Hear, O Israel, the Lord our God, the Lord is One!'

Shabbat (Sabbath)

Shabbat begins at sunset on Friday and lasts until sunset on Saturday. Shabbat means 'to rest'. It is seen as a gift from God. God created everything in six days and rested on the seventh and made it a holy day of rest. Preparations are done in advance. Some of the family attends the synagogue before the evening meal. Everyone dresses in their Shabbat clothes and the mother lights the candles and ushers in the Sabbath. The father blesses the children and reads from the scriptures.

On Saturday morning, families worship in the synagogue. The afternoon is usually a time for the family. At the end of Shabbat, a special candle is lit and everyone smells a box of spices. The hope is that the sweet smell of Shabbat will be remembered throughout the coming week. Shabbat is over when three stars appear in the sky.

Kashrut

Kashrut is the Jewish dietary laws. Food that meets these laws is known as kosher. Certain foods are forbidden (treyfah). Food allowed includes:

- any animal that has divided hoofs and that also chew the cud
- fish that has fins and scales
- insects that hop
- chicken, duck and turkey.

Meat and milk products may not be eaten or cooked together. Jewish kitchens have two sinks and two separate lots of utensils (one for milk and one for meat). All blood must be drained from the meat before it is eaten. The animals and birds must be slaughtered in accordance with Jewish law.

Most Orthodox Jews keep the kashrut laws but some Reform Jews are less strict.

Short questions

a   What is the Torah? (1 mark)

b   What is the Covenant? (2 marks)

Examination practice

a   What *two* features should an animal have to be accepted as kosher? (2 marks)

b   Explain the importance of Shabbat. (5 marks)

c   Explain the importance of the kashrut food laws for Jews today. (5 marks)

Checklist for revision

	Understand and know	Need more revision	Do not understand
I know about the origins of Judaism.	☐	☐	☐
I understand the importance of the Tenakh.	☐	☐	☐
I understand the Jewish beliefs about God and the Covenant.	☐	☐	☐
I understand Jewish beliefs about Repentance and the practices of Rosh Hashanah and Yom Kippur.	☐	☐	☐
I know about the kashrut food laws.	☐	☐	☐
I understand the importance and practice of Shabbat.	☐	☐	☐

SECTION A: KEY BELIEFS

6 Sikhism

What do I need to know?
- How Sikhism began.
- The significance of the Ten Gurus.
- The nature and significance of the Guru Granth Sahib.
- The nature of God.
- The Five K's.
- The Kurahit (prohibitions).
- Worship in the home and gurdwara.

Origins

Sikhism began in the fifteenth century in the Punjab. The term 'Sikh' means 'to learn'. The faith was revealed through the Ten Gurus.

key ideas
The Gurus are an example and inspiration to Sikhs. Their teachings help Sikhs live their lives in a way that is pleasing to God.

Guru Nanak (1469–1539)
The first guru was Guru Nanak who, when he was 30, dived into the river Bain and disappeared for three days. Sikhs believe he was with God. He set up the first Sikh community in Kartarpur. He taught that all people are equal.

Guru Angad (1504–52)
Guru Angad collected together Guru Nanak's hymns and some of his own. He encouraged sporting activities, as he believed a healthy body pleases God.

Guru Amar Das (1479–1574)
Guru Amar Das promoted the idea of hospitality and the community kitchen (the langar). He rejected the idea of social and religious class and caste.

Guru Ram Das (1534–81)
He founded the important Sikh city of Amritsar.

Guru Arjan (1563–1606)
Guru Arjan completed Amritsar, including the Harimandir (the Golden Temple). He formed the Adi Granth (the first version of the Sikh scriptures).

Guru Har Gobind (1595–1644)
Known as the warrior guru, he trained Sikhs to fight.

Guru Har Rai (1630–61)
He encouraged the offering of free medicines and medical care to the sick.

Guru Har Krishan (1656–64)
He was five when he became Guru. He died three years later of smallpox.

Guru Tegh Bahadur (1621–75)
He taught that everyone should worship God in whatever way they wish.

Guru Gobind Singh (1666–1708)
Guru Gobind Singh formed the Khalsa and said that the Guru Granth Sahib would be their living Guru.

Guru Granth Sahib (Adi Granth)

The words of the Gurus are written in Gurmukhi (the written form of Punjabi). It has 1430 pages (every copy is laid out in the same way). It includes 5894 shabads (hymns) arranged into 31 ragas (musical groupings). It teaches Sikhs to meditate on the Name of God and to lead purposeful lives. It is shown great respect.

The nature of God

The Mool Mantra outlines the nature of God.

'There is only one God
Truth is His Name (Satnam)
God is the creator
God is without fear
God is timeless and without hate
He is beyond birth and death
He is self-existent
He can be known by the Guru's grace.'

The Khalsa (Community of the Pure)

At Baisakhi in 1699, Guru Gobind Singh demanded that a Sikh should volunteer his head for sacrifice. Five volunteers were taken into the tent one by one. Each time, Guru Gobind Singh reappeared with blood running off his sword. Later, all five volunteers returned unharmed. Guru Gobind Singh gave them amrit to drink and the 'Panj Pyares' (the five beloved ones) became the first members of the Khalsa.

The Five K's

Guru Gobind Singh told members of the Sikh brotherhood to wear the Five K's.

- The kesh is the uncut hair. Because it grows very long, men wear turbans and women wear scarves to keep it tidy.

- The kangha is a small wooden comb Sikhs use to keep their long hair tidy.

- The kara is a steel bangle worn on the right arm or wrist.

- The kaccha are shorts, similar to a soldier's under-shorts.

- The kirpan is a ceremonial sword.

In modern Britain, some Sikhs choose not to wear all the Five K's; for example, some Sikh men trim their beards.

Kurahit (prohibitions)

Khalsa members keep the four prohibitions as set out in the Rahit Maryada (Sikh Code of Discipline). These are:

- do not trim, shave or cut one's hair
- do not use tobacco or alcohol
- do not eat halal meat
- do not commit adultery.

Worship in the home

Sikhs daily meditate on the Name of God. They reflect on God's names, for example, Waheguru (Wonderful Lord), Satnam (the Eternal Reality), and Akal Purakh (the Eternal One). The worshipper repeats the Japji (Mool Mantra). God is put at the centre of their lives.

A gutka (a collection of hymns) is used as an aid to worship. Sikhs believe in sewa (serving all people).

Worship in the gurdwara

There is no set day for diwan (worship) but most British Sikhs worship on Sundays. Worship includes singing, praising God, and reading the Guru Granth Sahib. Shoes are removed and worshippers bow or prostrate themselves before the Guru Granth Sahib and make an offering for use in the langar. They sit on the floor cross-legged. Men and women usually sit apart.

The Guru Granth Sahib is the focal point. It is placed on a takht (raised platform) under a palki (canopy), covered by fine clothes (when not being read). The granthi waves a chauri (fan) over it as a sign of its authority. A granthi may read it and give a sermon. During Ardas (final prayers) the karah parshad is mixed and then shared by everyone. This is 'blessed food' made of semolina, ghee, sugar and water.

The langar

The langar is a free kitchen and every visitor is welcome. After worship, Sikhs share a vegetarian meal. The Gurus taught that Sikhs should share their possessions. The gurdwara also acts as a community centre. Many hold lessons in Punjabi, clubs for senior citizens, and mother and toddler groups.

6 Sikhism

Short questions
a Which of the Gurus founded the Khalsa? (1 mark)
b Name the Sikh holy book. (1 mark)

Examination practice
a Give *two* ways the Guru Granth Sahib is shown respect. (2 marks)
b 'The gurdwara is like a community centre, not a place to worship.' Do you agree? (5 marks)
c Explain the meaning and importance of the langar to Sikhs today. (5 marks)

Checklist for revision

	Understand and know	Need more revision	Do not understand
I know about the origins of Sikhism.	☐	☐	☐
I understand the importance of the Guru Granth Sahib and the Ten Gurus.	☐	☐	☐
I understand Sikh beliefs about the nature of God.	☐	☐	☐
I know the Five K's.	☐	☐	☐
I understand the Kurahit.	☐	☐	☐
I understand the importance of worship in the home and gurdwara.	☐	☐	☐

SECTION A: KEY BELIEFS

7 Christian ethics: Attitudes to love and forgiveness

What do I need to know?
- How Christians make decisions.
- Types of love in the New Testament.
- Love – of God, neighbours and enemies.
- St Paul's concepts of love.
- Jesus' words and actions on forgiveness.

Decision making

Christians often find guidance from their religion when making moral decisions. The Bible is studied as God's living word. Other sources of authority are also consulted. These include the following.

- Tradition: over the centuries, the Church has established beliefs and teachings on many issues.
- Prayer: to ask for guidance to do the right thing.
- Church leaders: church leaders are asked for advice.
- Reason: the consequences of actions are considered.
- Conscience: this gives a sense of what is right and what is wrong.
- Example: Jesus' or other important Christians' (past or present) examples are copied.

Love

did you know? The New Testament includes four main types of love: agape, eros, philia and storge.

Agape is Christian love involving practical help.

Eros is sexual love or desire.

Philia is the love of friends and friendship.

Storge is warm affection or liking for something.

The Great Commandment (Mark 12: 28–34)

A lawyer asked Jesus, 'Which commandment is the most important?' Jesus replied, 'First, love God totally and secondly, love your neighbour as you love yourself.' Christians should put God first and, secondly, treat others as they wish to be treated.

Qualities of love (1 Corinthians 13)

St Paul described true love as being patient, kind, not jealous or conceited, or proud, or ill-mannered or selfish – love is eternal.

Love for enemies (Matthew 5: 43–8)

Jesus told his followers to love their enemies and pray for them.

The Parable of the Good Samaritan (Luke 10: 25–37)

Jesus told of a man who was mugged while travelling from Jerusalem to Jericho. A priest and Levite came by but did not help. A Samaritan stopped, poured oil and wine on the wounds and bandaged them. He took the man to an inn and paid for his care. 'Which had acted like a neighbour?' asked Jesus. 'The one who was kind,' replied the lawyer.

key ideas

Christian love (agape) demands that help should be given to any needy person, even enemies.

Forgiveness

key ideas

God forgives anyone who repents and asks for forgiveness providing they forgive others. The Lord's Prayer (Luke 11: 1–4) says: 'Forgive us our sins, as we forgive those who trespass against us.'

7 Christian ethics: Attitudes to love and forgiveness

The Parable of the Unforgiving Servant (Matthew 18: 21–35)

Peter asked, should he forgive his brother seven times? Jesus replied seventy times seven (meaning always). Jesus said a king's servant owed the king millions of pounds. The king decided to sell the servant and his family into slavery. But the servant begged for forgiveness and time to pay and the king generously forgave him his debt. This servant then threw another servant who owed him a few pounds into prison. The king was furious and had the unforgiving servant put in prison.

key ideas

The king represents God and the servant represents a sinner. God forgave the servant for all his wrongdoing, but when the servant does not show that same forgiveness to others then God's justice is shown.

The woman caught in adultery (John 8: 1–11)

A woman caught committing adultery was brought to Jesus. The Lawyers and Pharisees said, 'Shall we stone her as the Law of Moses demands?' Jesus invited anyone who had never sinned to throw the first stone. The religious leaders left one by one until only the woman and Jesus remained. Jesus said, 'I will not condemn you, go and do not sin again.'

key ideas

Jesus believed that all people are in need of mercy and forgiveness and he encouraged the woman to make a new start.

The healing of the paralysed man (Matthew 9: 1–8)

Some friends carried a paralysed man on a bed to Jesus. Jesus saw their faith and said to the man, 'Your sins are forgiven.' Some Lawyers whispered, 'Only God can forgive sins. This is blasphemy!' Jesus challenged them: 'Is it easier to say, "Your sins are forgiven," or to say, "Get up and walk"? To prove the Son of man's authority to forgive sins, I will heal the man.' The man was instantly healed.

did you know? Jews believed that some people become ill because God punishes sinners.

The Parable of the Prodigal Son (Luke 15: 11–32)

The younger of two sons asked his father for his inheritance then left home and spent his money recklessly. When a famine came, the only job available was feeding pigs. He got so hungry that he wanted to eat the pig food. Realizing his stupidity, he returned home. His father ran to greet him and hugged him. A new robe, sandals and a ring were brought. The prize calf was killed and a party organized. The older brother was furious. 'All I have is yours,' said the father, 'Come in and join the celebration.'

did you know? Working with pigs was a terrible job for Jews because they believed that pigs were unclean animals.

key ideas

The father represents God who is willing to forgive a repentant sinner. The younger son is a sinner who repents and the older brother the religious leaders who were unforgiving.

The crucifixion (Luke 23: 26–43)

Jesus was crucified with two criminals at the Place of the Skull. He prayed, 'Forgive them

Father! They do not know what they are doing.' Many people jeered Jesus, including one of the criminals, but the other told him to stop. He asked Jesus to remember him when he came as king. Jesus replied that today he would be with him in paradise. The criminal was sorry and received forgiveness.

key ideas

Jesus lived a life without sin. He took upon himself the sins of the world. He became the perfect sacrifice to pay for our forgiveness.

Short questions

a What is the first commandment? (1 mark)

b State *two* things that St Paul said about love. (2 marks)

Examination practice

a Name *two* types of love found in the New Testament. (2 marks)

b What does the Parable of the Prodigal Son teach about forgiveness? (5 marks)

c Explain what the Parable of the Good Samaritan teaches about love. (5 marks)

Checklist for revision

	Understand and know	Need more revision	Do not understand
I understand how Christians find guidance when making moral decisions.	☐	☐	☐
I know the types of love in the New Testament.	☐	☐	☐
I understand Jesus' and St Paul's teachings about love.	☐	☐	☐
I know and understand Jesus' words and actions on forgiveness.	☐	☐	☐

SECTION B: QUESTIONS OF MEANING

8 The existence of God

What do I need to know?
- The evidence for and against the existence of God.
- The **First Cause** argument.
- Arguments for and against **design** of the universe.
- Religious experience: illusion or reality?
- Types of religious experience: **conversion**, worship, prayer, miracles and meditation.
- What is meant by religious revelation.
- The meaning of **theist**, **atheist** and **agnostic**.

hints and tips
You should refer to *one* or *two* religions in this section.

did you know?
The major world religions (except for Buddhism) believe in a creator God.

People who believe that God exists are called theists.

People who believe that God does not exist are called atheists.

An agnostic believes that it is impossible to know if God exists.

The First Cause argument (St Thomas Aquinas)
- The universe itself is the best evidence for God.
- Everything in the world has a cause, so the universe must also have a cause.
- There had to be something eternal (without beginning or end) that was not caused by anything else.
- God is that eternal first cause.

A modern version: God caused the big bang that started the universe and eventually all life evolved from it.

Arguments against God as the first cause
- Just because events/things have causes, it does not mean the universe itself has a cause.
- The universe could have always existed (be eternal).
- It still does not answer 'who or what caused God?'

key ideas
Theists believe that God created the universe and life on earth for a purpose. The universe did not come about by accident or chance. Human beings are special because they have a special **responsibility** for God's creation.

Design of the universe
Nature is so intricate and complex that it must have been designed by God – it could not have happened by random chance.

Sir Isaac Newton's thumb
The thumb's design is so clever and unique to every individual, that it alone convinced Newton that there was a designer of the world.

action point
Write a sentence to explain how each of these shows good 'design':
- a snowflake
- the human body
- nature itself.

William Paley's watch

- William Paley compared the world to a watch found lying on the ground.

- If you had never seen a watch before, its intricate workings would convince you that it was designed. Cogs, wheels and springs could not have come together by themselves.

- The universe is even more complicated than the watch (for example, the human eye is more complex than a telescope, which can only help the eye) therefore must have had a designer – God.

Arguments against a designer

- **Evolution**: since the process of natural selection (the fittest survive, the rest die out) happens by chance, species really designed themselves.

But even in Darwin's day, people argued that God had started evolution knowing how it would turn out. Human beings, with such high powers of intellect and the capacity to create and be moved by great music, art and literature, could not arrive at such complexity entirely by chance.

- Design faults: if God designed the world, why are there so many faults in its structure (plates in the earth's crust move causing earthquakes, and so on)? The universe has always existed and continues to develop and change.

- Problem of evil: if God designed everyone and everything, why did God create evil? Why is nature so cruel?

Religious experience

Many people believe in God simply because they say they have experienced God personally in their lives. People say that God has been 'revealed' to them through such experiences and this may result in a conversion (change of belief).

Siddattha Gotama had a spiritual experience as he meditated under a bodhi tree. First he overcame a series of temptations and then he reached enlightenment.

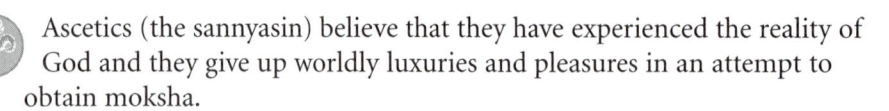

Saul (who became St Paul) was blinded by the light of Jesus on the road to Damascus and converted to Christianity (Acts 9: 1–12).

Ascetics (the sannyasin) believe that they have experienced the reality of God and they give up worldly luxuries and pleasures in an attempt to obtain moksha.

As Muhammad meditated in a cave on Mount Hira, the angel Jibril (Gabriel) appeared. Muhammad was told that he had been chosen by Allah (God) to be the last and greatest of all the prophets.

> ✓ **action point**
>
> You should learn *one* example of a conversion or religious experience/revelation from the religion(s) you have studied.

8 The existence of God

Moses (Exodus 3) experienced God in a burning bush.

Guru Nanak plunged into the river and did not surface again. After three days he appeared at the same spot from where he had disappeared. Sikhs believe that he had been with God.

There are many modern examples of revelation.

Religious experiences through worship

Some people claim to experience the presence of God as they worship.

When Roman Catholics receive Holy Communion, they feel God's presence inside them physically. Some Christian worship is **charismatic**, meaning 'filled with and led by the Holy Spirit'. Some claim to have been given spiritual gifts such as prophesying and speaking in 'tongues' (strange languages or sounds, which seem to pour out of the person).

key ideas
Religious believers say that God can be known and is 'revealed' through:

- nature
- the lives and work of religious leaders
- religious writings
- personal experience.

Prayer and meditation

Many worshippers claim that while praying or talking to God, aloud or silently, in public or in private, God has spoken to them. Many feel closer to a personal, **immanent** God. By talking to God like a friend, the relationship grows and they can share their hopes and problems with Him.

Meditation helps some believers to feel a spiritual presence. Distractions are pushed from the mind. A phrase may be repeated (a mantra) or a passage from the sacred writings studied.

By opening the mind and heart and really listening, revelations of God's word, peace and love may be received. Some claim to receive spiritual dreams or visions.

Buddhists meditate to focus on peace, love and tranquillity, and to gain insight.

Miracles

Many worshippers go on pilgrimages to holy sites seeking miraculous cures for illnesses. Some claim healing, from incurable diseases such as multiple sclerosis. For example, Christians may go to Lourdes.

A few years ago it was claimed that statues of deities in Hindu temples in various parts of the world started drinking milk, including at a temple in London.

The Jews claim that God fed the Israelites in the desert with manna and that he parted the Red Sea.

Are such experiences illusion or reality?

An atheist or an agnostic would say that such experiences/revelations are illusions (imaginary, not real) and are not good evidence for God's existence.

- Private experiences have no reliable outside witnesses.
- Public worship can be observed, but it is impossible to be certain what people are experiencing.
- It could be psychological phenomena – imagination, mass hysteria, tricks of the mind, wishful thinking, or hallucinations.
- Miracles have no apparent natural explanation but this does not mean that God brought them about.
- If someone said God spoke to him or her in a dream, you could say they dreamed God spoke to them – a very different matter.
- The person might be making the experience up.

A theist would argue that religious experiences/revelations are real and prove God's existence.

- Conversion really changes a person – others can see its effects.
- Prayer, meditation and worship have a deep impact on those who practise them – to them they are real experiences of God.
- Visions and dreams are very real to the person who experiences them. If God is within each person, He could inspire them to dream about God.
- Some healing miracles have been verified by doctors – the people who were healed know it was real.

> **action point**
> You should learn at least *one* example of a miracle from the religion(s) you have studied.

SECTION B: QUESTIONS OF MEANING

9 The problem of suffering

What do I need to know?
- Types of suffering: natural or man-made?
- The origins of suffering.
- Does suffering have a purpose?
- The meaning of **free will**.
- What questions does suffering raise about God's love and purpose?
- In what ways is suffering unjust?

hints and tips
You should refer to *one* or *two* religions in this section.

What is suffering?

Suffering may be described as anything that causes pain, grief or damage. It includes going through a bad time, experiencing hardship, distress, agony, misery, and anything that makes life unpleasant.

Suffering has occurred throughout history. Records reveal the horror of the slave trade, wars, epidemics, famines, and the cruelty of many dictators and rulers. Problems associated with injustice, genocide, disease, malnutrition and slavery still exist in the world today. Images of the planes crashing into the World Trade Centre in America on 11 September 2001, the war in Iraq or of starving children and those who are near to death in countries devastated by drought and famine spring to mind when considering those who suffer.

In our own lives we will have known sickness, pain, worry and unhappiness: times when we have suffered agony from injuries or broken relationships.

key ideas
Suffering is a 'problem' for everyone. All human beings experience pain, illness, loss and finally death.

Types of suffering

There are two main types of suffering – natural disasters and those that are the result of human action (man-made).

- Natural disasters: disasters that bring suffering that are caused by nature, for example, earthquakes, volcanoes, flooding, drought and crop failure (famine).
- Man-made: where people cause suffering through their actions. Sometimes these actions are deliberate and evil, for example, war, murder, theft and rape.

Sometimes reference is made to the following types of suffering:

- individual: where one person suffers, for example, from losing a loved one
- self-inflicted: where the suffering is the result of the person's own actions
- medical: where a person or group suffer because of disease or a disability
- community: where a district is affected by the suffering, for example, the closing of a major industry, famine or war.

Causes/origins of suffering

Suffering may result from accident, deliberate choice, evil, wrongdoing or sin. Causes include anger, craving, envy, greed, hatred, ignorance, laziness, lust, pride, selfishness and thoughtlessness. Suffering may be the result of:

- someone else's actions. For example, people suffer because of crimes such as rape, murder, theft or shootings.
- our own choices and actions. Our actions may have been done accidentally, deliberately or without knowing what we were doing (ignorance).
- nature or natural disasters. For example, people suffer because of floods and disease.
- unfortunate circumstances. For example, people suffer because they were born into a poverty stricken country.

action point
Which pictures show natural suffering and which show suffering caused by people? Give a reason for each choice.

key ideas
Suffering is a problem for believers in an all-good, all-loving, all-powerful, all-knowing God. It makes people question God's love, God's purpose and God's power.

9 The problem of suffering

Questions raised by suffering

- Why is there so much suffering in the world?
- Is it God's intention (purpose) to make us suffer? (If so, then God must be cruel.) Or does suffering just occur without God wanting it to happen? (If so, then God must be weak.)
- If God is all-loving and cares for us, why does God allow us to suffer? (If God wants us to suffer then God is not loving, God is cruel.)
- If God is all-powerful, God must be able to stop our suffering, yet suffering continues. (If God cannot stop our suffering then God is not powerful, God is weak.)
- If God is all-knowing, God must realize we suffer. Surely God's knowledge and power could be used to stop suffering? Why is it not?

How is suffering unjust?

Innocent suffering: people who have lived good lives or children who have not done anything wrong do not deserve to suffer.

Does suffering have a purpose?

- Not all suffering is pointless – pain tells us something is wrong with us so we can do something about it.
- Some people say suffering has made them a better or stronger person.
- Some suffer to achieve a goal, for example, a mountain climber or polar explorer.
- Some suffering helps others, for example, self-sacrifice during war.
- Suffering may be a test of a person's faith.
- Suffering may teach a lesson (it used to be thought it was a punishment for sin).
- Suffering may have a purpose (be part of God's plan) but we do not know what that purpose is.

Religious responses to suffering

Christianity

- Natural suffering is not God's fault – just part of the way the world has developed since its creation by God.
- Suffering caused by human beings occurs because God gave people free will. People are free to choose how to behave and sometimes choose actions that cause suffering.
- Christians believe Jesus made up for the sins of humans by his innocent suffering and death on the cross, so breaking the power of evil and suffering over humans.
- Trusting in God helps Christians to endure suffering.
- Christians accept personal suffering as God's (mysterious) will but will try to alleviate the suffering of others whenever they can.

> **action point**
> Write down three examples of suffering that you think are unfair or undeserved. Why is the suffering in each case unjust?

> **hints and tips**
> The story of the Fall (Genesis 3) explains how suffering and evil came into the world because of human disobedience. Adam and Eve then had to face the consequences of their free choice.

> **hints and tips**
> In the Bible, the book of Job gives three explanations for Job's suffering: it is a test of faith; it is a punishment for sin (which God rejects), and is part of God's purpose (beyond human understanding).

Buddhism

- The Buddha taught that life is unsatisfactory, full of frustration and suffering (dukkha).
- People suffer because of sickness, injuries, old age and death.
- The three 'poisons' of ignorance, greed and hatred lead to more suffering.
- The origin of suffering involves peoples' selfishness, greed and craving (tanha).
- The cure is to get rid of desire and craving and to discover inner satisfaction (niroda).
- The Buddha taught the Middle Way (magga).
- This is set out in the Eightfold Path – a path that leads to escape (nibbana).

Hinduism

- Suffering is the result of **paapa** (sinful actions) in this life and past actions in previous lives. Hindus believe that people reap what they sow (karma).
- It is important to build up good karma, as it will help reduce suffering in the future (**agami karma**).
- The goal should be to achieve moksha and escape from the cycle of birth, death and rebirth, and from suffering.

Islam

- Allah gave Adam the world to look after but also gave him free will, so humans can choose to sin.
- Satan (Iblis) was given the job of testing human faith.
- Suffering tests faith and character.
- If people cause suffering they will be judged on the Day of Judgement.
- Muslims should show compassion towards those who suffer.
- One of the 99 names of Allah is 'The Compassionate'.

Judaism

- Suffering results from free will.
- Adam and Eve brought suffering into the world by their choice to eat the forbidden fruit (Genesis 3).
- Jews suffered terribly through the Holocaust.
- Jews are encouraged to help those who suffer.
- Suffering is a way that God disciplines His people (Deuteronomy 8: 5).
- God uses suffering to bring people back to Him (Isaiah 53: 5).

Sikhism

- Ego and selfish human action (**haumai**) result in suffering.
- Actions in the physical world affect rebirth so it is important to do good.
- Suffering is the result of karma.
- It is the aim to rise beyond or transcend suffering.
- Some suffering is a mystery including why people suffer more in some parts of the world than people in other areas.

SECTION B: QUESTIONS OF MEANING

10 Life after death

What do I need to know?
- Evidence and reasons for belief in life after death.
- Reasons why some people do not believe in life after death.
- Beliefs about heaven and hell.
- Beliefs about reincarnation.
- Influence of a belief in life after death on people's lives.

hints and tips
You should refer to *one* or *two* religions in this section.

The evidence for life after death

Ancient beliefs

- Archaeologists say that 150,000 years ago, Neanderthal man practised ritual burial and appear to have believed in a spirit world and life after death.
- The Ancient Egyptians built pyramids and embalmed bodies in order to preserve their dead Pharaohs for life in the underworld.
- The Chinese emperor, Shih Huang Ti, who died around 210 BCE, was buried with 6000 terracotta soldiers, horses and chariots to protect him in the next world.

Ghosts and spirits

Many people believe in ghosts. They are said to be spirit apparitions through whom the souls of dead persons show themselves. Many believe in haunted houses and exorcists claim to be able to remove the spirits.

The presence of dead relatives

Some people say dead relatives have visited them and mediums claim to have made contact and received messages from the dead.

Near death experiences

Patients from different societies, cultures and religions, who have undergone major surgery, have claimed to have had near death experiences. These usually take one of two main forms:

- leaving their body, they were able to look down from the ceiling onto the bed to see the operation taking place.
- their spirit drifting along a tunnel towards a bright light and beautiful music. Some entered a garden and were greeted by radiant figures only to be told that

his or her time is not up and they have to return to life. Some have recognized a dead relative or an important person from their religious beliefs.

Religious beliefs

- Buddhists believe in the idea of 'again becoming' (or rebirth).
- Christians believe the resurrection of Jesus proves that there is life after death.
- Hindus believe that it is only the body that dies and not the soul (atman).
- Muslims bury the dead as they believe in a physical resurrection.
- Judaism teaches that death is not the end but there are a variety of beliefs about the world to come.
- Sikhs believe in the rebirth or reincarnation of the soul into another body.

Evidence against life after death

Historical evidence
Just because people have believed things for centuries, this does not make it right. People believed for centuries that the earth was the centre of the universe and that everything revolved around it and that the world was flat.

Ghosts or spirits
Many people have made up ghost stories. They could all be fairy stories. There may be other explanations for these sightings.

Presence of dead relatives
Many mediums have been proved to be fakes who prey on the person who wishes they could contact their dead relatives.

Near death experiences
Some scientists suggest that these 'so called' experiences may have other logical explanations. Perhaps the brain has a mechanism that is triggered near death that creates a sense of euphoria. Feelings of ecstasy can result from lack of oxygen to the brain. Could the images of an afterlife be the result of ideas stored in the brain during a person's lifetime?

The influence of a belief in life after death

The law of karma
Buddhists, Hindus and Sikhs believe that what they sow they will reap (the law of karma). Believers obtain as much merit as possible in order to benefit in future lives or escape the cycle of birth, death and rebirth.

> **action point**
> Develop a model essay giving arguments for and against a belief in life after death.

> **key ideas**
> Christians, Jews and Muslims believe that there is a Day of Judgement when they will have to account for their actions. Many people hope that the future life will be better than the present one. All the major religions encourage believers to help others and live a moral life. Many teach that good deeds and actions will bring rewards in the next life. Some teach that bad actions will bring punishment.

10 Life after death

Heaven and hell

Christians, Muslims and many Jews believe heaven (paradise) is a place of sheer delight and joy where:

- God/Allah lives
- God/Allah is worshipped
- the righteous will receive their reward for all eternity
- there are no tears or sadness.

Christians and Muslims believe that after death those who fail the judgement of God/Allah will be sent to hell.

In Islam, Jahannam (hell) is seen as a place of torment and torture without any hope of mercy. Some Christians believe it is a place of punishment with Satan and his demons. Others believe hell is being isolated from the presence of God. Many Roman Catholics believe in **purgatory** – a place between heaven and hell where people suffer to be cleansed of their sin before being allowed into heaven.

Jews believe that the unrighteous will be sent to **gehinnom** (hell). This is not a place of everlasting torment, but souls are cleansed from their sins so that they may enter the presence of God.

Reincarnation

Reincarnation is the belief that we may be reborn again after death. Sometimes this is into a lower life form and not as a human. Transmigration refers to the Hindu belief that the soul and spirit may be reborn into a human foetus or newborn child. Buddhists and Sikhs believe that they have had many lives before this one and that many of these were as lower life forms.

> **action point**
> Work out why the religion(s) you have studied teach that it is important to live a good life in this life.

Religious beliefs about life after death

Buddhists are encouraged to follow the teachings of the Buddha, read the scriptures, meditate, follow the Middle Way, and behave in a thoughtful way by showing loving kindness towards others. The karmic energy of a person sets another life in motion. Being reborn in a 'better' birth is seen as a steppingstone towards entering nibbana. Nibbana, the perfect ideal, is an eternal state beyond suffering and impermanence.

Christians teach that heaven is the reward for those who repent of their sins and accept Jesus Christ as their personal saviour and Lord. Jesus told his followers to store up riches in heaven, so Christians attend church, study the Bible, pray, and do good actions, for example, working for a charity, helping the homeless and the sick.

Hindus believe that if they follow the Laws of Manu and do their duties this

The Salvation army helping the homeless

37

will mean a good life in the future. Good karma that will affect their reincarnation can be achieved by following the path of yoga (meditation). There is every encouragement to lead a good life, worship the deities, read the holy books, go on pilgrimage, and perform good deeds. The aim is to obtain moksha and be joined with Brahman and escape the cycle of birth, death and rebirth.

Islam stresses the importance of morality and preparing for the Day of Judgement. Muslims worship Allah because he resurrects the dead. They pray, fast, attend the mosque, follow the teachings of the Qur'an, give zakah, and perform good actions.

There is hope of resurrection and immortality. Faith in God is vital and will be rewarded. Jews believe there will be judgement, so a good life and good actions are important. The cleansing of the souls of the unrighteous in gehinnom (hell) may last for up to a year. Jews look forward to the Messianic Age when the Messiah will reign. Preparation includes worshipping the one true God, following the Torah, attendance at the synagogue and praying.

Sikhs rely on the grace of God but they believe that it is important to follow the guidelines laid down in the Rahit Maryada (Sikh Code of Discipline). The aim is to break free from the cycle of death and rebirth and achieve mukti or liberation. Death is another step towards ultimate unity with God. To help achieve this, Sikhs believe they should worship at the gurdwara, read the Guru Granth Sahib, pray, and do good actions, for example, sewa (service).

SECTION B: QUESTIONS OF MEANING

Examination questions

Using bullet points is fine for revision, but you will lose marks if you use them in the exam.

Examination type questions

a What reasons for believing in life after death might religious people give? (6 marks)

b 'There is no such thing as life after death.' Do you agree? Give reasons for your answer, showing that you have thought about more than one point of view. (5 marks)

Student's answer

a Christians believe that there must be life after death because Jesus came back to life again. St Paul wrote to the Church at Corinth saying that it would not have been possible for Jesus to have been resurrected if life after death did not exist. Also, if Jesus came back to life so can his followers through belief in him. There have been claims by people that they have died, spoken to Jesus in heaven and returned to life again or had a near death experience where their spirit left their body.

b It is difficult to know for certain if there is life after death. Certainly people have believed in an afterlife since ancient times and Christians point to the resurrection of Jesus as proof. But it is something that cannot easily be proved. Ghosts, near death experiences and the like may have other logical explanations. Perhaps Jesus did not really die or maybe the whole story was made up by his followers to upset the authorities.

Personally, I cannot discount the possibility, but if there really is life after death, I will never know for certain until I die. If there is not then I will never know for sure.

Examiner's comments

a A good example of Jesus and the idea was developed. Also, near death experiences and coming back from the dead was mentioned, but the answer could have been further developed. Mark: 3/6

b Arguments for and against are included and the difficulty in obtaining proof is clearly evident. Reference is made to Christian teaching. If the ideas were developed further it would have received top marks. Mark: 4/5

Short questions

a	What is a theist?	(1 mark)
b	Explain, using examples, what is meant by religious experience.	(5 marks)
c	What is 'man-made' suffering?	(2 marks)
d	Give *two* ways religious believers can help those who suffer.	(2 marks)
e	Explain what is meant by near death experiences.	(2 marks)
f	Explain what is meant by reincarnation.	(2 marks)

Revise for GCSE Religious Studies AQA B: Key beliefs, ultimate questions and life issues

Remember to include religious teachings/beliefs as well as secular points in your answers.

Examination practice

a Explain the argument for the existence of God based on design of the universe. (5 marks)

b 'If God exists there would be no suffering.' Do you agree? Give reasons for your answer, showing that you have thought about more than one point of view. (5 marks)

c What reasons might religious people give for believing in God? Give reasons for your answer, showing that you have thought about more than one point of view. (8 marks)

d What problems are raised for religious believers by suffering? (5 marks)

e Explain what life after death will be like according to the teaching(s) of the religion(s) you have studied. (7 marks)

Checklist for revision

	Understand and know	Need more revision	Do not understand
I know the First Cause argument.	☐	☐	☐
I know the arguments for God's existence based on design of the universe.	☐	☐	☐
I know the meaning of the terms theist, atheist and agnostic.	☐	☐	☐
I know the argument for God's existence based on religious experience.	☐	☐	☐
I understand why some people think religious experiences are illusions.	☐	☐	☐
I understand why suffering is a problem for believers in God.	☐	☐	☐
I know the difference between natural and man-made suffering.	☐	☐	☐
I understand the causes/origins of suffering.	☐	☐	☐
I know and understand why religious people say that suffering can have a purpose.	☐	☐	☐
I know the meaning of free will.	☐	☐	☐
I understand how religious faith can help people respond to or face suffering.	☐	☐	☐
I understand the reasons why some people believe in life after death.	☐	☐	☐
I understand the reasons why some people do not believe in life after death.	☐	☐	☐
I understand the beliefs about heaven and hell and reincarnation.	☐	☐	☐
I understand the influence of a belief in life after death on people's lives.	☐	☐	☐

SECTION C: LIFE ISSUES

11 Abortion

What do I need to know?
- What **abortion** is and what the law says about it.
- Why a woman may want an abortion.
- Why people are in favour (pro-choice) or against abortion (pro-life).
- When does life begin?
- The **sanctity of life**.
- The **quality of life**.
- What religion(s) say about abortion.

exam watch

In your exam, make sure you answer the question that is asked – do not just write down everything you know about abortion.

hints and tips

You do not need to know the medical details about abortion but should know what British law says about abortion.

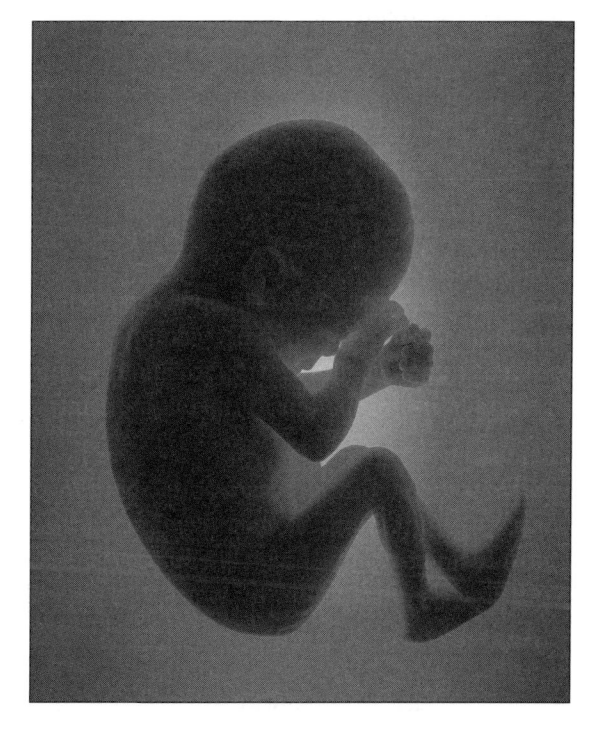

What is abortion?

A good definition of abortion is:

'The removal from the womb of a growing **foetus**, whether it is tiny or well developed and recognizable as a growing human being.'

What does the law say about abortion?

According to British law (other countries may be different), an abortion cannot take place after twenty-four weeks of pregnancy unless there is a serious risk to the mother's life or if the foetus is severely handicapped. There are four conditions – at least one of which must apply if an abortion is to be allowed:

1. The pregnancy risks the life of the mother.
2. The pregnancy poses a risk to the mother's physical or mental health.
3. An additional child could pose a risk to the physical or mental health of any children in the existing family.
4. There is a serious risk that the child will be born severely physically or mentally handicapped.

Two doctors must agree to the abortion and it must take place in a specially licensed clinic or hospital.

Why might a woman want an abortion?

There are many reasons why a woman may want an abortion. Most of them are allowed under the mental health aspect of condition 2 (above). This risk to the mother's mental health may be due to the woman thinking she is too young to be pregnant or by the pregnancy being a result of rape or an accident. The woman thinking she is incapable of bringing up a child, perhaps because her partner has left or she cannot afford a baby, may also cause mental problems.

Why are people against abortion?

People against abortion are said to be 'pro-life'. They usually believe that the foetus is alive in the womb so aborting it is the same as killing it. Many religious people are against abortion because they believe it is against God's wishes. They believe life is sacred and humans do not have the right to take this life away (sanctity of life).

- Buddhists believe that life begins at conception. Abortion is interfering in the cycle of death and rebirth. It is allowed, however, if the motive is not selfish.
- Most Christians (especially Roman Catholics) believe abortion is wrong because it goes against the sanctity of life. Some Christians believe that if it is more loving for an abortion to take place, it is allowed depending on circumstances.
- Hindus believe that abortion is wrong because it goes against ahimsa (non-violence) but will be allowed if life is threatened. Abortion affects the woman's karma, especially if the motive is wrong.
- Muslims believe that abortion is allowed in the case of rape or if the mother's life is in danger. Allah has a plan for everybody and abortion goes against this plan. In the first 120 days of pregnancy, the mother's rights are greater than those of the foetus so this is when abortions should occur. At 120 days, the foetus gains a soul.
- Jews believe that abortion is wrong because of the sanctity of life, but it is allowed if the mother's or baby's life is in danger, or if the pregnancy is the result of rape. Some Jews allow abortion if the mother's mental health is threatened.
- Sikhs believe that abortion is only allowed in the case of rape because life comes from God. However, parents have the right to choose in the case of a severely handicapped child.

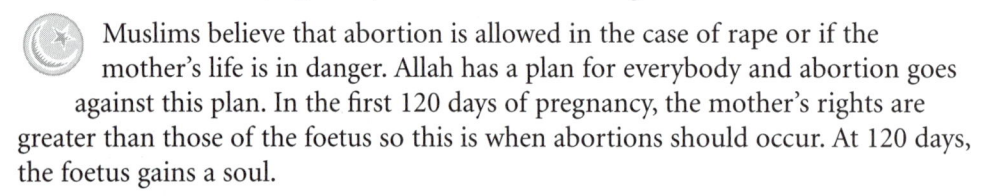

No one knows the potential of the child. An aborted foetus could have been another Einstein, Mozart or Beckham. Most people against abortion believe life begins at conception, or at least early on in the pregnancy, so they think the foetus has the right to be born. It is alive and nobody has the right to take that life away. If abortion is freely allowed, it could be used as birth control, which would be selfish and in most people's eyes, wrong.

Why are people in favour of abortion?

Supporters of abortion are usually said to be 'pro-choice'. This means they believe that the woman has the choice to decide whether or not she wants an abortion. The decision is hers alone, although she may be offered advice. They think that:

did you know?
Twenty-three weeks after conception, the foetus has all its organs and looks like a baby.

exam watch
If you are asked to explain why a woman may want an abortion, explain the reasons, do not just list them.

key ideas
Sanctity of life is important in any life issue. It is only relevant to abortion if the foetus is thought to be alive.

action point
Find and learn a relevant quote about abortion from the religion(s) you have studied.

- the foetus is part of the woman's body
- she will have to carry the child for nine months and then give birth to it
- she will feed and nurture the child once born
- she has a natural and emotional attachment to her child.

For these reasons, she has the right to abort the foetus. The father may offer advice, but in the end he has no rights in making his partner keep the child.

Whilst none of the major religions support pro-choice groups, most do allow abortion in some circumstances (see key ideas on page 42).

One of the biggest arguments in favour of abortion refers to the quality of life. If the child faces a poor quality of life for any reason, for example, being handicapped or unwanted, a pro-choice believer would say it is more humane to deny the foetus life because it would be preventing it from the suffering it would experience if born. A more religious view of the quality of life includes being able to live in dignity, free from pain, and in a way God wants them to.

When does life begin?

This is the key question and one that no one can answer with any certainty. Most religions (Christianity, Hinduism, Judaism and Sikhism) believe it starts at conception although there is disagreement about this within each religion. Many Buddhists believe life starts before conception because of the cycle of samsara (birth, death and rebirth) whilst Muslims believe the child has a soul at 120 days after conception.

However, some Muslims believe it is alive before this time. If life does begin at conception or soon after, abortion goes against the rule that all religions have about not killing. This also fits in with the sanctity of life. However, if life begins later in pregnancy or at birth, such arguments do not apply.

hints and tips
Sanctity of life is usually used as an argument *against* abortion and quality of life is usually used as an argument *for* abortion.

exam watch
Use ideas about when life begins to support your arguments for and against abortion.

SECTION C: LIFE ISSUES

12 War and peace

> **What do I need to know?**
> - Some details about war to use as examples.
> - The link between religion and war and peace.
> - The cost of war – financial, human and environmental.
> - Why people fight – **just war** theory, **holy war**.
> - Alternatives to fighting.
> - What religion(s) say about war and peace.

Details about war

Wars have happened throughout history and they are happening at this moment. The growth of the media in the twentieth century brought war into every home in Britain, especially wars in which we were involved either as a nation or through the United Nations.

Recent wars include the Gulf War in 1991 when the United Nations declared war on Iraq because Iraq invaded Kuwait, and the war on terrorism focusing on Afghanistan as a result of the World Trade Centre attack on 11 September 2001. In 2003, the war between a coalition of countries led by the United States of America and Great Britain against the regime of Saddam Hussain in Iraq was broadcast on news channels twenty-four hours a day for several weeks.

Links between religion and war and peace

All religions stress that we should live in peace with each other.

- Hinduism and Buddhism stress ahimsa (non-violence). Living life in a non-violent way will help their reincarnation to a higher level.
- Sikhism tries to promote harmony between religions but Sikhs will fight to defend their beliefs. They will not be the aggressor trying to gain more land.
- Christianity, Islam and Judaism stress peace but will fight under certain conditions. These conditions are a just war and a holy war (see page 44 and 45).

Despite this teaching about peace, religions have been involved in war throughout the centuries. From the eleventh to thirteenth century, Christians and Muslims fought in wars called the Crusades, which were inspired by their beliefs.

hints and tips
Do not give too much detail about specific wars; just use them for examples.

Current terrorist problems are partially blamed on religion whether Christianity in Northern Ireland, Islam in Afghanistan and the Middle East, or Judaism in Israel. In some cases, religion is only a label to persuade believers to follow the actions of a few.

The cost of war

- Financial: war is expensive. Global military expenditure is over £100 million per hour.
- Human: millions of people die in wars (more than 100 million people died as a result of war in the twentieth century).
- The environment: war causes pollution. Towns, cities and rural areas are all affected. Nuclear war will cause devastation to the environment.

Why do people fight?

There are many reasons why people fight:

- to defend their country, religion or way of life
- to defend another country, religion or way of life
- to take over another country
- to remove their own government or leader (Civil War).

These are not necessarily reasons that are acceptable to all people but you need to know them!

Just war

This idea was first put forward by a Christian called St Thomas Aquinas in the thirteenth century. It was added to later but Aquinas is given the credit for it. 'Just' means being fair, right or acceptable. It gives six circumstances and if all six are met, Christians believe it is acceptable to fight. Most other religions agree with this (with a few subtle differences) but Buddhism teaches it is never right to fight. The six circumstances are:

1. war must be started and controlled by a proper legal authority
2. a just cause is required (those who are attacked must deserve it)
3. the reason must be to advance good, not evil
4. the war must be a last resort (other ways of solving the problem tried first)
5. there must be a good chance of success
6. the fighting must be proportional – excessive force should not be used and civilians must be protected.

Even though these ideas are very old, they are still used today by both religious and non-religious people.

Holy war

The idea that God helps people to win battles and wars is a very old one. Jews believe that they would never have been able to occupy the Promised Land of

---

exam watch

Remember, in your exam you can only include *two* religions in any one answer.

did you know?

Over 60 per cent of the soldiers fighting in World War I died.

Canaan in around 1200 BCE if God had not helped them. The Battle of Jericho is a good example of this. Muslims and Christians both believe that God was helping them during the Crusades.

There are usually three elements to a holy war:

1. the war must achieve a religious goal
2. a religious leader must authorize the war
3. people taking part are promised a spiritual reward (probably life after death with God or a higher reincarnation) if they die in a holy war.

Reasons for a holy war might be to spread their faith, to defend their faith, or to reclaim holy places or followers captured by faithless enemies. If people believe they are fighting for their God, they may be better motivated in their fighting as they become more fearless due to the reward they are offered.

Many believers of all religions are not happy with the idea of a holy war. Holy wars are rarely just wars. In recent times, terrorists claiming to be Muslims have unsuccessfully tried to declare a holy war against enemies to try to persuade their fellow people to join their struggle.

key ideas

Just war and holy war are useful if you are answering a question about why religious people may fight.

Alternatives to fighting

For some people, no amount of argument about just war and holy war will persuade them to fight. The belief that fighting is wrong is called **pacifism**. Religious pacifists follow their religious ideas about not killing or not harming any living thing (ahimsa). In the past, some classed such people as cowards, but now they are given the term **conscientious objectors**. This acknowledges that their reluctance to fight is due to their beliefs rather than cowardice.

Many of these people take part in war, not by fighting but by doing vital (and often dangerous) support jobs like stretcher carriers, ambulance drivers or labourers.

did you know?

In World War II there were 59,000 conscientious objectors in Britain.

Some religious ideas

The idea of the sanctity of life is very important here. All religions believe life is special. For all religions except Buddhism, this is because life comes from God and therefore should not be taken by anybody except God. Buddhists believe that life is special, as all living things have to be given the chance to be reincarnated at a higher level. They should have every chance to gain good karma to do so.

'Do not kill' from the Ten Commandments (Exodus 20: 13) or 'Do not harm any living being' (the first precept in Buddhism) are also important teachings. Hindus use the belief of ahimsa (non-violence), as do Buddhists and Sikhs (although Sikhs can fight in self-defence or defence of their faith).

The Christian teaching of 'love your neighbour' (Matthew 22: 39) could be used to justify fighting in defence of somebody else, even another country. The result of the fighting may be more loving to the people you are fighting for than the method used.

exam watch

Use the religious ideas relevant to the religion you are studying in your exam.

SECTION C: LIFE ISSUES

13 Prejudice and discrimination

What do I need to know?
- The difference between **prejudice** and **discrimination**.
- Different types of prejudice.
- Why people are prejudiced.
- Tolerance.
- What can be done about prejudice.
- What has been done about prejudice.
- What religion(s) say about prejudice and discrimination.

key ideas

Prejudice is an attitude; discrimination is an action linked to prejudice.

What is prejudice?

Prejudice means to think badly of someone because of their race, religion, colour, gender, and so on. It is not based on any good reasoning and can be extremely destructive when it inspires actions. An action inspired by prejudice is called discrimination.

A person who discriminates on the grounds of prejudice tends to treat everybody of a particular race, colour, and so on, the same, regardless of their individual qualities or failings. All religions are against prejudice although there are plenty of examples of religion seeming to be prejudiced, especially with regard to their attitudes towards other religions and towards women.

did you know?

Around 6 million Jews were murdered during World War II because Hitler was prejudiced against them.

Different types of prejudice

Racism

This is the attitude that people of a certain race are inferior. People with this attitude tend to treat people from this supposed inferior race badly. It may even lead to murder. If done by a country, it can be very destructive, as it has been in countries like Kosovo and Iraq, where a great many people from certain races in these countries have been murdered. This is called 'ethnic cleansing'.

Sexism

If a person is discriminated against because of their gender (that is, whether they are male or female), this is called sexism. It has been common in the past for women to be discriminated against by men who have had the power to do this. This has led to women being left to look after the home whilst their husbands have done 'more important things'. As a result, many women have been denied the chance to develop and use their talents for the good of all.

exam watch

If answering a question on prejudice, start by briefly writing what prejudice is.

Religious prejudice

Although all religions are against prejudice, sometimes their attitudes towards other religions are prejudiced. This comes from an opinion that their religion is superior. Religious prejudice, however, can also happen when a person with no religious beliefs is prejudiced against either a believer or a particular religion.

Social prejudice

Usually the rich in society being prejudiced against the poor.

Ageism

Some elderly people feel they are discriminated against (as do some young and middle-aged people) because of their age.

Homophobia

This is when a person feels they are discriminated against because they are homosexual (gay).

Why are people prejudiced?

Some people believe that there cannot be any good reason for prejudice. However, people have given the following reasons so you should know and understand some of them.

- They may have had a bad experience at the hands of someone from the group they are prejudiced against.
- A prejudiced person may also be the victim of prejudice.
- People learn attitudes and opinions from their family. This may include prejudice.
- Lack of education can cause prejudice.
- A group may be made into scapegoats. This means they are blamed for a particular problem (wrongly) and are mistreated as a result. This happened to the Jews during World War II.

Tolerance

This is the opposite of prejudice. It means to be tolerant of people different from you and accept them as people with the same rights, feelings and needs as yourself.

Responses to prejudice

Religious teaching is against prejudice so it follows that religious believers should be against prejudice. In the past, religion has not always practised what it preaches, especially with regard to women. Traditionally, women have not been allowed to be religious leaders, possibly because prejudiced men would not respect their work and opinions.

Attitudes in most religions are changing, but they still exist (for example, in the Roman Catholic Church, Orthodox Judaism and most Islamic sects). Differences between religions have often been emphasized and fought over, but nowadays several groups exist to understand and encourage tolerance towards people of other faiths.

---

action point
Think about whether you have faced any prejudice and discrimination. If so, think about how it made you feel.

action point
Look at the reasons opposite and decide whether you agree they are good reasons or not. Think why.

exam watch
If answering an evaluation question about prejudice, when giving a different view, use the idea of tolerance.

Perhaps the two best-known individuals whose religion has inspired them to protest against prejudice are Martin Luther King (Christianity) and Mohandas Gandhi (Hinduism) see table below.

Name	Martin Luther King	Mohandas Gandhi
Religion	Christian	Hindu
Dates	1929–68	1869–1948
Main country lived in	United States of America	India
Prejudice opposed	Racial	Social – the caste system
Methods	Peaceful protest; civil disobedience; political	Peaceful protest; civil disobedience; political
Most remembered for	Protest marches; 'I have a dream' speech	Identifying himself with the poor – leading them
Death	Assassination	Assassination

did you know? 3 million people took part in Gandhi's funeral procession.

Religious teachings about prejudice and discrimination

Divisions that may lead to prejudice are all illusory; at enlightenment there is no division between male and female. All members of the sangha, including women, are considered equal.

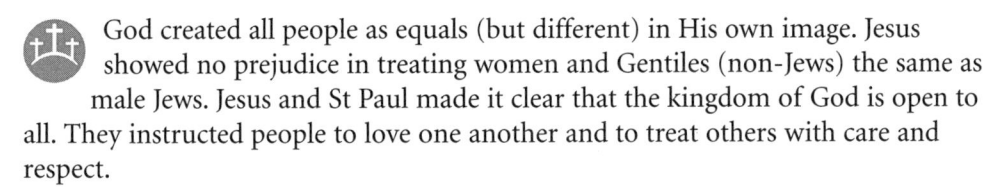

God created all people as equals (but different) in His own image. Jesus showed no prejudice in treating women and Gentiles (non-Jews) the same as male Jews. Jesus and St Paul made it clear that the kingdom of God is open to all. They instructed people to love one another and to treat others with care and respect.

All are equal in the sight of God and Hindus have a duty to treat all people with respect. This creates good karma. The caste system encouraged prejudice but is now illegal.

Equality is emphasized: Allah created all living things with differences, which should not be used as an excuse for prejudice. Paradise is available equally to all Muslims. The Qur'an teaches that prejudice should not be tolerated.

God created all people as equals (but different) in His own image. People should be treated with compassion regardless of differences between them. God's law applies to everybody.

All are God's children and so must be treated equally. All religions worship God so they must be treated with respect. Social differences should not lead to prejudice.

SECTION C: LIFE ISSUES

Examination questions

hints and tips

If you are answering from two religions, try to include a similar amount from each.

Examination type questions

'Peace cannot be kept by force; it can only be achieved by understanding.' (Albert Einstein)

a Explain why some religious people are pacifists. (6 marks)

b Give some of the conditions that must be met for a just war and explain what they mean. (9 marks)

c 'Peace cannot be kept by force.' Do you agree? Give reasons for your answer, showing that you have thought about more than one point of view. Refer to religious teachings in your answer. (5 marks)

Student's answer

a Pacifists are people who do not believe in fighting. Some religious people are pacifists because they believe that fighting is the wrong way to solve a dispute. Because of this they will not take part in a war. They believe in the sanctity of life, so to take someone's life away is wrong. Buddhists believe in ahimsa, which means that they should not kill so they will not join in a war even if it threatens their religion. Instead they may help out by doing things that do not involve fighting. Christians believe the parts in the Bible that say 'you shall not kill' and 'love your neighbour'.

b The just war is an idea that was first put forward by St Thomas Aquinas who was a Christian. It says that all of several conditions have to be met if a war is to be allowed. For example, there has to be a good reason for the war; it must not just be to gain land from another country. It must promote good and not evil. In other words, if the reason is seen as a bad one, the war would not be allowed. All other ways of solving the problem must have been tried, such as talking to the opponent before the war started and taking economic sanctions. During the fighting, civilians should not be targeted and weapons of mass destruction should not be used because they will kill a lot of people including women and children. If these conditions all apply, the war can take place and must finish when it has been won.

c I agree that peace cannot be kept by force. If you have armed soldiers in a country, they are not going to be able to keep peace because people might attack them. This would especially be the case if the soldiers came from another country. People would fight fire with fire and use the excuse that the soldiers are armed to fight. You can only have peace if nobody has weapons and all people do not want to fight. This will never happen so there is no point getting rid of weapons. On the other hand, if people have more weapons than you, you are less likely to fight because there is a good chance you will get killed.

Examiner's comments

a This answer gives a reasonable explanation of why people are pacifists and includes some good religious teachings. To earn more marks, it would need to explain what the sanctity of life and ahimsa means and apply the two biblical teachings to pacifism. Mark: 4/6

b This answer is quite good. It includes some of the conditions for a just war and explains them with examples. However, not all the conditions are included and the explanations are not detailed enough for more marks. If it did not explain any of the conditions, it could be given 4 marks at most, even if all the conditions were included (without explanation). Mark: 6/9

c This answer is not balanced although it does have a brief alternative opinion. There is no reference to religious teachings so full marks would not be possible. A conclusion would have been useful. Mark: 3/5

Examination questions

key ideas
In an evaluation question, give a balanced answer and a conclusion.

exam watch

Make sure you read the question carefully and more than once to make sure you answer what the question asks.

Examination practice

a Explain the reasons why a woman might want to have an abortion. (6 marks)

b Explain the religious teachings and beliefs that may help a woman decide whether or not to have an abortion. (9 marks)

c 'The rights of the unborn child should always be protected.' Do you agree? Give reasons for your answer, showing that you have thought about more than one point of view. Refer to religious teachings in your answer. (5 marks)

Checklist for revision

	Understand and know	Need more revision	Do not understand
I know and understand what British law says about abortion.	☐	☐	☐
I know and understand what *two* religions say about abortion.	☐	☐	☐
I know the meaning of sanctity of life and quality of life.	☐	☐	☐
I know what *two* religions teach about war and peace.	☐	☐	☐
I understand the criteria for a just war and I can explain why *one* war is just.	☐	☐	☐
I understand the concept of a holy war and I can give an example.	☐	☐	☐
I know about *two* of these forms of prejudice and discrimination in detail:			
• colour/race	☐	☐	☐
• gender	☐	☐	☐
• religion	☐	☐	☐
• age	☐	☐	☐
• class	☐	☐	☐
• disability	☐	☐	☐
• nationality.	☐	☐	☐
I understand the reasons why some people may be prejudiced.	☐	☐	☐
I understand what tolerance is and how people can show it.	☐	☐	☐
I know what *two* religions teach about prejudice and discrimination.	☐	☐	☐

SECTION D: PLANET EARTH

14 The origins of life

What do I need to know?
- Religious views about how life began.
- Scientific views about how life began.
- How the ideas can be combined.
- What these views teach us about how we should treat the planet.

hints and tips
You do not have to believe an idea or story to be able to write about it in your exam (if asked to).

All religions (except Buddhism) tell us about how the earth came into being and how life first started and then developed. The ideas were told and later written in the form of stories so people without any scientific knowledge could understand and remember them better. This is one of the reasons why many people find it difficult to believe them or accept that they could contain some 'truth'. No one has yet been able to prove any theory about the origin of the planet and life on it, whether religious or scientific.

The key point in all religious creation stories is that God created the earth. The method He used varies from one religion to another. Scientists cannot tell us why the earth was created and cannot include God in their theories. If they did include God in their theories, they would never be able to prove them because no one can prove that God exists. This is the biggest difference between religious and scientific ideas.

key ideas
In all religious creation stories (except Buddhism), God created the earth and everything on it. Science believes it happened by chance.

The biblical story of creation

Perhaps the best-known creation story is the one in the Bible. It is part of Judaism, Christianity and, with a few changes, Islam. It is written in the first book of the Bible, Genesis. It says the earth was made in six days with God resting on the seventh day. The story says that in the beginning, the planet existed (without telling us how). The rest of the story tells us how it was made fit for life and then how life was put on the earth.

Day 1 Light and dark
Day 2 The sky and sea
Day 3 The land, trees and plants
Day 4 The sun, moon and stars
Day 5 Sea creatures and birds
Day 6 Land animals and human beings
Day 7 God rested.

After each day, God was said to be pleased with his work because it was good.

After this story, the Bible gives us more detail about the creation of humans by saying that God created a man and woman called Adam and Eve. The implication

did you know?
This story was first written down between 3000 and 3500 years ago.

14 The origins of life

is that all humans are descended from Adam and Eve. Their disobedience brought evil and suffering into the world.

Although the Qur'an does not go as far as telling us a story of creation, it makes it quite clear that Allah created the earth and everything on it and is in control of His creation. The Bible's idea that this was completed in six days is echoed in the Qur'an. It also tells us that man (Adam) was created before woman (Hawa) and that we are all descended from these two people.

There is more than one creation story in Hinduism. This one is perhaps the best known. It starts with the God Vishnu asleep on a cobra (Ananta), floating on an ocean. He was woken by a humming noise (Aum) and then a lotus flower grew from his navel. The creator god Brahma was sitting in the lotus and on Vishnu's command divided the flower into three parts to make the heavens, the earth and the sky. He then made grass, plants, animals, birds, fish, and then people.

Buddhism does not have a creation story. The Buddha refused to answer questions about how the earth was created because he believed there is no simple answer that is right for everyone. Buddhists believe that worlds evolve and follow a cycle of birth, death and rebirth.

Sikhs do not have a specific creation story but they believe God created the universe and we can see evidence of Him in His creation. We cannot know everything about creation because human knowledge is limited.

exam watch

If Buddhism is the only religion you have studied, if asked about religious creation stories, make the point opposite and then it would be helpful if you learnt and used another creation story.

What does science say about the earth's origins?

Most scientists have similar ideas about how the earth was created although they may disagree over some of the details. They think that around 10 billion years ago, there was a massive explosion somewhere in the universe. The result of this explosion is the universe as we know it. Our solar system came later when the conditions became right for it to begin. This is called the **Big Bang** theory.

As the earth cooled, life appeared. It started in the sea and eventually life on land appeared, with humans evolving from apes as the final (for now) and most developed species. Nowhere in the scientific theories is there an answer about *why* this process happened.

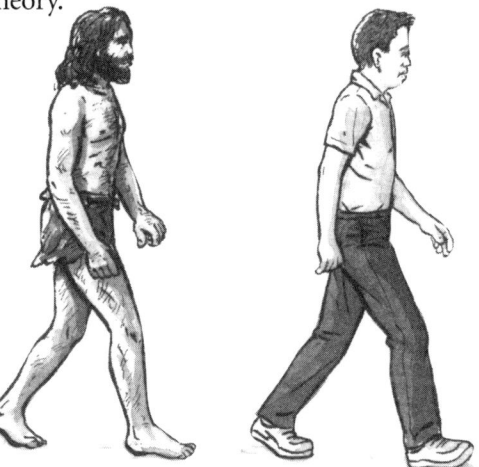

did you know?

Scientists believe the effects of the big bang are still being felt at the outer reaches of the universe.

Can we put both ideas together?

Some people believe that the scientific theories tell us the methods God used to create the earth. He started the process (and maybe created the conditions for the Big Bang to happen). The rest happened naturally. The religious stories do not tell us about these methods but deal with the question about why the earth was created and why life was put on the earth – a question that science does not try to answer.

What does religion tell us about caring for the planet?

All religions except Buddhism believe that as God made the earth, we have the responsibility to look after it for Him. Christianity, Islam and Judaism believe that God put us on the earth for this very reason. They think we are **stewards** (or khalifahs in Islam) of the earth. The earth belongs to God and we are looking after it so we should do all we can to make sure it is not mistreated. This includes the way we treat other living things and issues such as pollution and deforestation.

Hindus believe that looking after the earth is a duty and results in good karma, whilst Sikhs see evidence for God in creation so they should respect it. Even though Buddhists do not believe in a creator God, they insist the earth should be looked after and no living thing should be harmed.

> **hints and tips**
>
> If answering an evaluation question about how the earth was created, use both the religious and scientific ideas and then combine them.

SECTION D: PLANET EARTH

15 Human attitudes towards animals

What do I need to know?
- The difference in value between animals and humans.
- The rights of animals compared to humans.
- Vegetarianism, factory farming, animal experimentation, hunting.

What is the difference between animals and humans?

Apart from the obvious physical differences, there are other more important ones.

- Humans are on a 'higher level' than animals. This is especially true for people who believe in reincarnation.
- It does not appear as though animals are able to think as we do.
- Animals cannot make rational decisions; they act on instinct (for example, survival, hunger, and so on).
- Humans can appreciate things like art, music and beauty, and express an opinion about them. This opinion can then be communicated to other humans.
- Humans create societies that protect the weaker members. For animals, survival of the fittest seems to be more appropriate.
- Animals do not have religion and do not seem able to communicate with God.

Whether animals have a soul depends on personal belief. People who believe in reincarnation (Buddhists, Hindus and Sikhs) believe that when a body dies, the soul takes a new body, which can be from the animal kingdom. Religions that believe in heaven and hell (Christians, Jews and Muslims) tend to think that animals do not have a soul and the afterlife belongs only to humans.

None of this means animals can be mistreated. However, some people feel that humans have the right to use animals for their own benefit. We use animals for a lot of things (food, clothing, to work for us, to entertain us). Some people do not think we should do any of this; others are happy for us to use animals for anything that does not harm them. The problem arises with using animals for food.

Should we eat meat?

Around 90 per cent of people in Britain eat meat although some eat only 'white meat', for example, poultry. Those that do not eat meat are called **vegetarians**. There are several reasons given for being a vegetarian.

- The principle behind raising animals and then killing them for meat is cruel.
- The way some animals are raised and then killed is cruel. 'Factory farming' seems to show little regard for the animals' welfare.
- Humans can eat a meat-free diet and still be healthy.
- We do not have the right to kill animals.

exam watch

If asked about the difference between animals and humans, use some of these ideas, not flippant ones; for example, animals have four legs!

beware

You cannot use arguments about reincarnation unless you are using at least one religion, that is, Buddhism, Hinduism and Sikhism, in the maximum of three religions you are allowed.

Revise for GCSE Religious Studies AQA B: Key beliefs, ultimate questions and life issues

A small proportion of people not only refuse to eat meat, they will also not use any product that comes from an animal, for example, leather and dairy products. These people are called vegans.

Meat eaters think differently.

- Animals were provided on earth for us to eat.
- We have canine teeth, which are designed for chewing meat.
- Meat is an excellent source of protein.

Religious views on vegetarianism

Religion has mixed views on vegetarianism.

Most Buddhists are vegetarian. Their belief in ahimsa (non-violence) includes animals. Animals are part of the cycle of birth, death and rebirth, so they must not be mistreated. Killing an animal could be killing the body that houses the soul of one of their ancestors.

Some Christians are vegetarians. The Bible tells Christians that animals were put on the earth for people to use. Jesus was not vegetarian: we know he at least ate fish. Despite this, the cruelty aspect of killing animals for food persuades some Christians that it is wrong to eat meat.

Most Hindus are vegetarian. Their reasons are similar to Buddhist ones. However, some Hindus will eat some meat but never from the cow, as this is a sacred animal.

Muslims eat meat although they have strict rules about what they eat. Meat they can eat is called halal and includes lamb, beef and chicken. Pork and shellfish are not allowed. Animals that are eaten have to be killed by slitting the throat and draining the blood out. While they are killing the animal, the Shahadah is recited.

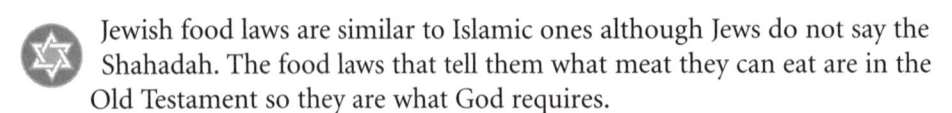

Jewish food laws are similar to Islamic ones although Jews do not say the Shahadah. The food laws that tell them what meat they can eat are in the Old Testament so they are what God requires.

Many Sikhs eat meat although it is not served in the langar (communal kitchen in the gurdwara) in case it is offensive to Sikhs who do not eat meat. Many of the Gurus were hunters and ate meat.

Animal experimentation

Many people who eat meat are against using animals to test products on. Some think it is all right to test medicines on animals but not cosmetics. The drug insulin, which is vital to many people with diabetes, was developed using some ingredients derived from pigs and also tested on animals. Others are either against testing in all circumstances whilst many people accept that it is necessary to make sure people can trust products they use.

Some companies like The Body Shop and Beauty Without Cruelty have used the fact that their products are not tested on animals as successful marketing ploys. Nowadays, many products carry the slogan 'not tested on animals'.

action point
Look carefully at the arguments opposite. Try to think of alternative arguments for each one.

key ideas
Only Judaism and Islam have direct teachings on whether meat should be eaten or not (via their food laws, although some Jews and Muslims choose to be vegetarians). The other religions decide by applying more general principles.

See Kashrut in Judaism on page 19.

Why does it matter?

Opponents of animal experimentation believe it is cruel to animals and that we do not have the right to harm them for our own purposes. Supporters point to the idea that animals were put on the earth for us to use and through testing, provide benefit to humans so it is acceptable, despite the cruelty. Certainly the development of some medicines has been helped by animal experimentation.

What does religion say?

Whilst founders of religions and sacred writings do not say anything about animal experimentation, religious teachings can be interpreted to come up with ideas about it. Most of the general teachings about vegetarianism apply to testing, as do the ideas about the relative value of animals and humans. Basically, no religion is in favour of unnecessary testing, but Christianity, Islam and Judaism generally accept it. Buddhism, Hinduism and Sikhism are against testing because of the harm it causes to animals, but many individual believers are prepared to use products that have been tested on animals.

Hunting, shooting and fishing

It is considered traditional for people to gain enjoyment from hunting animals. Nowadays, mainly foxes, shooting animals and 'game birds', and fishing. Some people call these activities 'blood sports' because they kill or at least injure other creatures. There are arguments for and against these activities.

Arguments in favour

- They are traditional country activities.
- They keep down the population of pests.
- They help to conserve the countryside.
- Some activities limit the spread of disease.

Arguments against

- They are cruel to other living creatures.
- As methods of conservation and pest control, they are of limited value.

Religions tell us little about hunting, shooting and fishing. The ideas above are relevant. Some of the Sikh Gurus were hunters and Jesus is said to have eaten fish. The idea of stewardship is relevant. However, it can be used on both sides of the argument: if it is useful for conservation, it is good stewardship!

> **did you know?**
> Around 85 per cent of animals used in experimentation are either mice or rats bred specially for the purpose.

> **did you know?**
> Fishing is the biggest participation sport in Britain.

> **key ideas**
> Animals and humans are different. People were put here to look after the animals (stewardship) and use them for our own purpose.

SECTION D: PLANET EARTH

16 The care of the planet

What do I need to know?
- How we respond to four environmental problems.
- Pollution, including global warming.
- The use and abuse of natural resources.
- Destruction of natural habitat.
- Animal and plant extinction.
- Religious teachings on care of the planet.
- The Assisi Declaration.

hints and tips
If you know about pollution from geography or science lessons, use this learning to help you give an informed answer about pollution. Do not forget religious attitudes, though.

Pollution

There are four main types of pollution.

Type	Example of causes	Example of effects
Land	Disposal of waste in 'landfill sites'; litter; careless use of fertilizer and pesticides	Illness of humans and other wildlife; inability to grow crops that are safe to eat
Air	Smoke from industry and houses; harmful chemicals being released into the air; exhaust fumes from transport	Breathing problems for living things, including people with asthma
Water	Waste being disposed of in rivers and the sea; water running off polluted land or draining into underground streams; oil spills	Harm caused to creatures that live in the water; drinking water made unsafe
Noise	Industry; selfish use of radio, TV, and so on	Hearing problems; poor quality of domestic life

Why is pollution so bad today?
- A more affluent, consumerist way of life leads to us wanting more and better things. Pollution could be a result of their manufacture.
- The earth's population is increasing quickly. There are now more than 6 billion people on earth.
- Some people do not care about pollution and causing it.

did you know?
In Britain, industrial pollution is heavily controlled by law. However, pollution is not restricted by national boundaries.

16 The care of the planet

Global warming

One of the most serious ways the future of the earth is being threatened is by global warming. This is caused by a growing imbalance in the atmosphere. The amount of carbon dioxide in the air is increasing. This is due to:

- burning coal and oil to produce electricity
- the cutting down of trees at a massive rate means more carbon dioxide and less oxygen (trees 'breathe in' carbon dioxide and release oxygen).

The effect of this is that more heat is trapped inside our atmosphere, leading to possible climate change. This could cause more droughts in some places and flooding in others.

The use and abuse of natural resources

The earth provides everything we need to survive. Most religions believe this is because God designed and created it for us. However, our technological way of life means we are using up many things the earth provides.

- We are using up non-renewable resources like coal, gas and oil. Once they are used up, there will be no more. If we cannot find other ways of generating power, we will have to adapt to do without it.
- Although the earth is capable of providing food for everybody, methods of farming in some poorer parts of the world are damaging the land and making it less likely that it can be used efficiently in the future. They are more susceptible to the effects of flooding or drought, which kills crops.
- The clearance of the rainforest often produces land that is not good enough to grow crops so it is wasted.

None of these examples show good stewardship (see page 54) and could lead to the destruction of the planet.

The destruction of natural habitat and the extinction of species

This is another potential problem caused mainly by the destruction of the rainforest. When such a clearance takes place, all sorts of species of wildlife lose their homes. This can cause a fight for survival, which is often lost. Once a complete species is wiped out, it will never reappear. This may be a species that could be useful to us in the future – it may even be a species we have not yet discovered. Wiping out a species may also affect the food chain, which could lead to the extinction of other species.

Species are becoming extinct in other ways as well. Most of these are down to the actions of people. Uncontrolled hunting has threatened some of the earth's most beautiful animals, including tigers. Disease, pesticides and weedkillers also contribute to various species of wildlife becoming extinct.

---

did you know? In the next 50 years, the earth's population is predicted to rise by more than 50 per cent.

action point For more information, use the Internet. Try searching for Greenpeace and Friends of the Earth.

read more See the section on stewardship on page 54.

What does religion say?

Much of the religious teaching is included in the sections on the origins of life and animal issues.

- The idea of stewardship is a key one; that is, God made the earth for us so we should look after it for Him because it is His earth; we do not own it.
- Obviously, any action that causes harm to another living thing is against teachings about not being selfish and loving and caring for and respecting living creatures.

In 1986, representatives of conservation agencies and religious leaders met at Assisi to discuss the state of the planet. Each religion produced a statement in support of conservation of the planet.

There is a striking similarity between exterminating the life of a wild animal for fun and terminating the life of an innocent human being at the whim of a more capable and powerful person.

Christians refuse to be associated with all ill-considered exploitation of nature that threatens to destroy it and, in turn, to make man the victim of degradation.

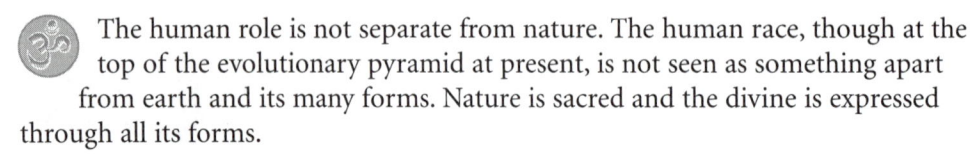

The human role is not separate from nature. The human race, though at the top of the evolutionary pyramid at present, is not seen as something apart from earth and its many forms. Nature is sacred and the divine is expressed through all its forms.

His [Allah's] trustees [all Muslims] are responsible for maintaining the unity of His creation: the integrity of the earth, its flora and fauna, its wildlife and its natural environment.

Now, when the whole world is in peril, when the environment is in danger of being poisoned, and various species, both plant and animal, are becoming extinct, it is our responsibility to put the defence of nature at the very centre of our concern.

A human being needs to derive sustenance from the earth, not to deplete, exhaust, pollute, burn or destroy it.

> **did you know?**
> In the twentieth century, 90 per cent of the world's tiger population died out and there are now breeding programmes to prevent their extinction.

SECTION D: PLANET EARTH

Examination questions

Examination practice

a Explain why many people think that humans are superior to animals. (6 marks)

b A young person has to decide whether to take a job in a laboratory that carries out experiments on animals. Explain how religious beliefs and teachings might influence this person's decision. (9 marks)

c 'No one should hunt animals for pleasure.' Do you agree? Give reasons for your answer, showing that you have thought about more than one point of view. Refer to religious teachings in your answer. (5 marks)

Student's answer

a I think that humans are superior to animals because we can do things they cannot do. Religious people say that God made the earth and that people were made after animals to look after them. If we look after them, that makes us better than them. We can also think and make decisions.

b If the person was a follower of Christianity or Islam, they would not work in the laboratory. Both religions say that animals should not be harmed. Christians believe that God made the earth. Humans were made last and were told to care for the animals that God also created. This is called stewardship and means that we should not do anything to harm an animal. However, some Christians would take the job because it will let them help people. Muslims also would not work here. They believe that Allah created the earth and made people khalifahs to look after it. The Qur'an also would not allow it. They might allow testing for medicines because they are important, but not cosmetics.

c I agree that no one should hunt animals for pleasure. Not only is it cruel to hunt them, it also goes against what religions teach. We do not have the right to hunt animals. They have not done us any harm and they do not try to hunt us! How would hunters like a twenty metre fox chasing them until they are exhausted and then killing them? I think people who hunt animals are cruel. The Bible tells us to look after animals, especially in the creation story. If God wants us to look after animals, we should not chase them and kill them. This is not what God wants. It may have been all right in the past, but we are more civilized and advanced now so we should not do it.

Examiner's comments

a This answer gives a reasonable explanation but needs more examples. It says that people can do things animals cannot do but does not say what. The religious reference is good but it would be better if it identified the religion(s) it comes from. Mark: 3/6

b This is a reasonable answer. The statement that both religions say animals should not be harmed is very general. The answer correctly mentions that Christians are stewards and Muslims khalifahs but does not go into much detail. The final Christian statement about helping people is good but needs developing, perhaps with a simple quote. There are teachings in the Qur'an that do not permit cruelty to animals – including one would have been a good idea. The final point is perhaps true but needs some explanation. The main weakness is that it lacks specific beliefs and teachings. Mark: 4/9

c This seems to be quite a good answer. It includes several points and has some religious teachings. However, it is completely one sided – there is no alternative point of view (the question requires this for full marks). A completely one-sided answer can only be given 3 marks. This one probably deserves 3 marks because it shows understanding with a detailed argument. Mark: 3/5

Revise for GCSE Religious Studies AQA B: Key beliefs, ultimate questions and life issues

If asked for religious beliefs and teachings, make sure you include some and not just generalized attitudes.

Examination practice

a How is human activity threatening the future of the earth? Give examples. (6 marks)

b Explain what religious beliefs and teachings tell us about why we should protect the earth. (9 marks)

c 'If religious believers looked after the earth well, so would people who do not believe in religion.' Do you agree? Give reasons for your answer, showing that you have thought about more than one point of view. (5 marks)

Checklist for revision

	Understand and know	Need more revision	Do not understand
I know one creation story in detail.	☐	☐	☐
I know one scientific theory of how the world was created.	☐	☐	☐
I understand what creation stories tell us about caring for the earth.	☐	☐	☐
I understand the concept of stewardship.	☐	☐	☐
I understand the difference in values between animals and humans.	☐	☐	☐
I know the religious attitudes to vegetarianism in *two* religious traditions.	☐	☐	☐
I know the attitudes to animal rights in *two* religious traditions.	☐	☐	☐
I know what *two* religions teach about the natural world.	☐	☐	☐
I know reasons why believers in *two* religions should care for the environment.	☐	☐	☐

Glossary

Abortion The practice of ending a pregnancy by operation

Agami karma Obtaining merit that will help to reduce suffering in the future

Agape Christian love

Agnostic Someone who believes that it is impossible to know whether God exists

Ahimsa Teaching about non-violence or non-injury found especially in Hinduism

Akhirah Life after death (Islam)

Anatta Buddhist idea that means 'no separate self' or 'no permanent identity or soul'

Anicca Buddhist belief that everything changes, nothing is permanent

Artha Economic development. The second human aim in Hinduism

Atheist Someone who believes that God does not exist and that it is meaningless to claim there is a God

Barzakh State of waiting after death for judgement (Islam)

Big Bang A scientific theory about how the universe came into existence

Charismatic (in Christian worship) Filled with and led by the Holy Spirit

Conscientious objector A person who will not fight in a war because of their beliefs. A pacifist

Conversion To change attitudes or beliefs and become a believer of a particular religion, for example becomes a Christian

Day of Judgement The day when God will judge peoples' lives

Design The argument for God's existence based on the intricacy, beauty and interdependence of life and the universe

Dharma Hindu idea of personal duty or righteousness

Discrimination Actions as a result of prejudice

Dukkha Buddhist word for suffering and that which is unsatisfactory

Eros Sexual love, affection, passion and desire

Evolution Theory that says living things change gradually over a long time

First Cause The argument that, since everything has a cause, God is the first cause of the universe

Foetus Fertilized ovum over eleven weeks once organs have developed

Free will The ability to choose or decide one's own actions

Gehinnom Jewish term for hell where the unrighteous souls go for cleansing

Haumai Sikh term for ego and selfish human action that causes suffering

Holy Trinity Holy belief in God the Father, Jesus and the Holy Spirit

Holy war Fighting for a religious cause controlled by a religious leader

Immanent (about God's nature) That God is present in and involved with life on earth and in the universe

Jahannam Muslim name for hell

Just war (from Christianity, Judaism or Islam) Conditions some follow to decide whether or not to fight

Ka'bah The House of Allah in Makkah

Kama Term for pleasure or desire

Karma In the Eastern faiths, the law of cause and effect. The sum of a person's actions in their life, which affects the next reincarnation

Magga Buddhist idea to live according to the Middle Way

Makkah The city in Saudi Arabia where Muhammad was born. It contains the sacred Kaaba

Meditation To think deeply and quietly. There are different forms particularly practised by Eastern religions

Miracles An unexpected (but maybe hoped for) positive event that appears to be impossible and is attributed to a supernatural power, for example a healing of an 'incurable' disease

Moksha (in Hinduism) Liberation from the cycle of birth, death and rebirth

Mosque Muslim place of worship. It means 'place of prostration'

Muezzin The man who calls the faithful to prayer

Nibbana (in Buddhism) The extinction of self and liberation from the cycle of birth, death and rebirth

Niroda Buddhist idea that the cure for suffering is to get rid of desire and craving

Paapa Hindu term for actions that are sinful

Pacifism The idea that fighting is wrong

Philia Love of friends

Prayer Method of speaking and communicating with God. It may include praise, thanksgiving and requests

Prejudice Thinking badly of someone because of the group he/she belongs to

Purgatory In Roman Catholic and Orthodox belief it is a place where souls go to be cleansed of their sins

Quality of life The idea that whether life is, or is going to be, good or bad should influence whether they live or die

Rak'ahs Actions made during Salah (Muslim prayer) consisting of recitations, standing, bowing and prostration

Responsibility Being accountable for one's own actions; a duty of care for others

Samsara Cycle of birth, death and rebirth in Buddhism and Hinduism

Sanctity of life Belief that life is precious because it comes from God and therefore should not be taken away by any person

Shruti 'What is heard' or 'revealed'; Hindu scriptures – Vedas and Upanishads

Smriti 'That which is remembered'; Hindu scriptures

Stewards People responsible for and looking after something on behalf of another (for example, humans caring for the created world on behalf of God)

Storge Warm affection or liking for something

Tanha Desire or thirst (second of the Four Noble Truths)

Tawhid The oneness of God

Theist A person who believes that God exists

Ummah The Muslim brotherhood or community

Vegetarians People who will not eat meat

Worship Action to show praise of an admired being, especially God

Wudu Muslim ritual wash before prayer

Index

abortion 41–3
agnostics 27, 30
ahimsa 13, 42, 44, 46, 56
Allah 16
animals 55–7, 59–60, 61
atheists 27, 30
atman 12

Bible 9-10, 24–6, 33, 52
Brahman 12

creation 27–8, 52–4

death 10, 16, 35–9
design of universe 27–8
discrimination 47–9

environment 54, 58–60
evolution 28

first cause 27
food 13, 19, 22, 55–7
forgiveness 24–6
free will 33–4

Gurus 21, 29

heaven and hell 16, 37, 55
Holy Communion 10, 29
Holy Trinity 9

Jesus 9–11, 15, 24–6, 33, 37, 56

karma 13, 34, 36, 38, 46

laws 15, 18, 19, 41, 56
life after death 10, 16, 35–9

life origins 43, 52–3
love 24

meditation 8, 14, 21, 29
miracles 29–30
monotheism 16, 18
Muhammad 15
Muslims 15–17

prayer 16, 19, 24, 29, 38
prejudice 47–9
prophets 15

Qur'an 15–16, 53

reincarnation 12, 36, 37, 46
repentance 9, 19
resurrection 9–10, 36, 38

samsara 13, 43
science 28, 53
shruti 12
Siddattha Gotama 6, 28
smriti 12
souls/spirits 12, 16, 36, 37, 55
suffering 6, 7, 31–4

Tenakh 18
theists 27, 30
Tipitaka 6

universe creation 27–8, 52–4

vegetarianism 13, 22, 55–6

war 44–6, 50